D0761745

Piping Hot!

Piping Hot!

Tales of a Wandering Bagpiper

Susan Hadley Planck

MOONSCAPE
PUBLISHING LLC

Piping Hot! Tales of a Wandering Bagpiper

Copyright © 2016 Susan Hadley Planck

All rights reserved.

Note: Some names have
been changed to protect the innocent … and guilty.

Books may be purchased by contacting the publisher, MoonScape Publishing, LLC, or author through the website at: SusanPlanck.com

Cover Design: Nick Zellinger (NZ Graphics)

Interior & E-Book Design: Nick Taylor (Light and Sound Graphics)

Publisher: MoonScape Publishing, LLC

Editor: John Maling, Judith Briles, Peggie Ireland, Andrew Planck

Manuscript Consultant: Judith Briles (The Book Shepherd)

ISBN 978-0-9908769-2-2 (Print)

ISBN 978-0-9908769-3-9 (E-Book)

Library of Congress Catalog Number: 2015914196

1) Adventure   2) Music   3) Travel

First Edition Printed in USA

To my kind, patient, fellow-traveler, Andrew Planck,

author of his own book,

What's Hot on the Moon Tonight?

Contents

1

WHY?

I blew and blew, and blew some more. Nothing! No sound at all, save the spits and squeals from my mouth.

"So, what d'ya wear under that thing anyway?" This most often asked question to a bagpiper has elicited many time-honored responses, from "socks and shoes" to the risqué, "A small set of pipes—care to blow?" These answers work better if you're a male, obviously. In fact, many bagpipers, following the time-honored Scottish tradition of "going regimental," wear nothing whatsoever under their kilts.

I finally gathered up my courage and decided to give the tradition a try. Of course, that was the evening when

I was sipping a beer at a fellow piper's house, and he and his friend decided to check out if I was, indeed, a true piper. After they brazenly lifted my kilt, I rethought my decision. Needless to say, I never went "regimental" again.

> There is a primordial sensual texture to the music infusing the entire body.

There truly is no other sound like the Scottish Highland bagpipes. There is a primordial sensual texture to the music infusing the entire body. Some listeners are moved to tears of joy while others are simply moved, with fingers in their ears, to leave the room in a fruitless effort to block out the sound. People seem to either love the pipes or hate them.

One lovely fall day I was playing my bagpipes a fair distance from the edge of a campground in Colorado's Rocky Mountain National Park when a woman came charging at me shaking her fists, screaming "Turn those things down!" My only way of "turning those things down" was to move farther away.

Another time, while climbing in the Japanese Alps with a small group, and having reached our goal for the day, I took out my pipes and played. One exhausted member of the group, with tears of happiness streaming down her face, said the sound helped inspire her to continue and reach the top!

Bagpipes were, indeed, classified as "an instrument of war." In fact, kilted Scottish soldiers fought with such ferocity in World War I that the Germans called them "The Ladies from Hell." The sound of the pipes has caused entire armies to retreat in defeat before the battle even began.

Imagine you are awaiting battle on a cold fog-filled morning, wondering if you will live to see that evening. Absorbed with fear and unable to discern the enemy because of the Scottish mist, you suddenly hear the skirling of a large group of untuned bagpipes coming your way. The sound is deafening bloodcurdling, and indescribable to the uninitiated. One can imagine that entire armies would drop their weapons, turn tail, and dissolve into the wilderness.

It has been said that each set of bagpipes is worth 100 guns in battle. They have been used in wars from Europe to Africa, Asia and America. Indeed, Nero may have been playing bagpipes instead of a fiddle when Rome burned. A World War I veteran from Britain stated, "When they played the bagpipes, I felt like I could get through anything." Sadly, more than 1,000 bagpipers fell in battle from 1914-1918.

Various forms of bagpipes exist in Spain, Hungary, Pakistan, Ireland, France, Bulgaria and other places. A crude form of a bagpipe can be traced to ancient Egypt.

Some of these bagpipes in other countries have only one or two drones as opposed to the well-known

Serbian bagpipes, one of more than 100 different types of bagpipes Photo @2005 by Nicola Smolenski. Knez Mihajlova Street, Belgrade.

Scottish bagpipes that have three. Some have a bellows to fill the bag instead of the player's breath. There are different shapes and sizes. The bag was originally the stomach of a goat or sheep!

The bagpipe has evolved to the point of becoming synthetic, complete with plastic reeds and a bag made out of Gortex—yes, the same material used in raingear. And what may have been African wood and ivory has been replaced in some instances with plastic as well. Word of caution: if you are an American piper, you must be wary of taking your ivory mounted pipes abroad. Customs officials are only too happy to confiscate them upon your re-entry to the United States.

No matter how much experience they might have in blowing other musical instruments, budding pipers will struggle initially. And, believe me, the "blowing" jokes around bagpiping are endless. But what I lacked in musical ability, I made up for in persistence, which is something we bagpipers need a lot of.

For endless months, I struggled to learn the intricate fingering techniques on a practice chanter. The recorder-like instrument was my sole companion while I longingly looked at my bagpipes resting in the case, laughing at my crazy attempt to get comfortable with the complicated fingering of bagpiping, waiting for the day I could actually try the real thing.

Since I had just divorced and moved to Boulder, Colorado, I was living the free and easy single life, working some part-time jobs, and had the time to devote to learning the pipes. Finally, after nine months, a lot of practice, and much pleading, I convinced my instructor to allow me to pick up the actual pipes.

Bagpipes have four reeds: single reeds in each of the three drones and a double reed in the chanter. And any one of these reeds alone is difficult to blow. Together, they require special technique as well as hearty lungs.

Many experienced pipers would dispute this, claiming from their lofty perch that I overstate the situation. There is, perhaps, a touch of snobbery in this attitude, or they just plain forgot what it was like when they began. The three drones, once tuned, should maintain a steady tone throughout all the tunes. Any wavering is the mark of a beginner. The chanter provides the nine melody notes.

With corks plugged in the three drones so I would only have the one double reed in the chanter to contend with, I anxiously blew up the bag. I blew and blew, and blew some more. Nothing! No sound at all, save the spits and squeals from my mouth. Drool formed and dribbled onto my shirt. I was devastated. It couldn't be that hard!

I tried again, this time holding onto the blow stick near my mouth, helping to create a seal. Squawk! It was a pitiful sound, but a sound nonetheless. I was ecstatic! I had just experienced the first of many rapid mood swings that all pipers experience, regardless of their ability, dependent on how their playing is going on any given day.

The instrument takes patience and extreme determination. I would need several more weeks before I could play a sound with all three drones uncorked. In spite of the God-awful squeals I was making, I was excited to be able to produce genuine bagpipe sounds.

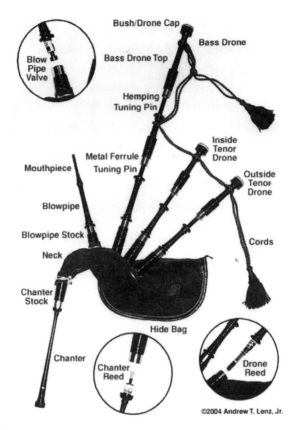

Details of the Highland bagpipe (Image copyright Andrew T. Lenz, Jr., BagpipeJourney.com. Used by permission)

A less than understanding relative who heard my first feeble attempts likened the sound to sticking a needle into a pig. He was not one of the bagpipe's greater admirers. Yet I love the sound. I enjoy challenges, and learning the bagpipes certainly was one of the greatest challenges I've ever faced. Perhaps bagpiping was also a way to compensate for the frustration I felt at never being heard at the dinner table as the youngest of five children. But I always found myself torn between the embarrassment and the enjoyment of the attention.

I suspect I'm a closet masochist. The instrument is just too difficult and frustrating for any sane person to tackle. If your fingers finally start to behave properly, the instrument may choose that day to develop its own contrary personality. The weather, time of day, and phases of the moon seem to affect the reeds.

Some chanter reeds last several months, others only a few hours. And then there was my friend who had spent several weeks breaking in her reed to just the strength she wanted it. As she showed it to her instructor and turned, she walked smack into the door with reed in hand. She looked at the smashed reed and burst into tears.

Bagpiping is not for the faint of heart. I've seen experienced, well-respected pipers throw their $2,000 pipes on the ground after a particularly poor performance in competition. I've seen

> ... playing the bagpipes quietly or unobtrusively is impossible.

pipers work for five years only to discard the pipes for good after being beaten by a talented 13-year-old with only two years of experience.

I do not consider myself an exhibitionist in any sense of the word, yet playing the bagpipes quietly or unobtrusively is impossible. I admit to enjoying the positive attention a bagpiper can receive—most of the time. A resident of Sidney, Nebraska, where our band played for more than twenty years at its Oktoberfest, approached us after one performance with the gratifying comment, "You have given us so much joy these past years." That may be what it's all about.

2
SHAKY BEGINNINGS

My heart just was not into teaching again, at least right away, but I had no other profession. And I had nowhere to go, geographically or otherwise.

What could lead someone almost 40 years old to take up bagpiping? The cause was more than a little convoluted and traumatic.

My divorce was final, and I remained in Washington state for the first year after the divorce where I had taught 3rd and 4th grade in the 120-student K-12 school for eleven years. I needed that year to regroup and convince myself that my best course was to move on. Where would I start my new life? After tiring of driving around the Northwest looking for a port in the storm, I found myself in Boulder, Colorado.

For fourteen years my husband and I had lived next to his mother's guest ranch in a beautiful secluded valley at the base of 12,300-foot Mt. Adams. We were a couple that "had it all": a spectacular self-designed house complete with barn beams; an unobstructed view of the volcanic, glaciated mountain towering 10,000 feet above us; my job teaching at a local school just a mile way—close enough to ski to in winter; a climbing school built from the ground up and molded into a successful business of ten years; and my husband's potential of high earnings as a sea captain. We had liked doing a lot of the same things: hiking, skiing and traveling. And we had similar values, an important attribute that helps cement long-term relationships.

After years of running our climbing school, we witnessed Mt. St. Helens erupt in 1980. The Forest Service subsequently closed the area on Mt. Adams, the dormant volcano 30 miles away, which halted our climbing operations. The access to Mt. Adams for more than a year was closed. After the stresses of the previous ten years of trying to keep people safe in the mountains, we would not reopen our climbing school the following year when people were again given access to the area.

Meanwhile, my husband had re-entered the marine world. Graduating from the Merchant Marine Academy, he had sailed as second mate before we'd met. Now his interest in the sea recaptured him. He began signing onto oceanographic research vessels that would take him out to sea for up to six months at a time and, eventually, to the rank of captain. Such absences did nothing to bolster an already shaky marriage. Of course we had discussed all of these potentially dangerous pitfalls and assured ourselves that we were not susceptible to them.

However, after several years of increasing absences, it became evident that we were, indeed, vulnerable to such pitfalls. I realized one day that I was not looking forward to his return. I had to face the unhappy reality that I preferred to be alone. In spite of his protestations to the contrary, I believe he had some misgivings about our relationship as well. We divorced soon after that, and I have no doubts that it was a good decision for both of us.

In the summer of 1985, I left the house that I had dedicated hundreds of hours to building: splitting cedar shakes for the roof; hauling basalt rock for the fireplace; routering two-inch Douglas fir planks for ceiling and floors; and carrying lumber until my arms matched those of a weight lifter. The house had been our creation, and we'd lived there for more than ten years. Now I was leaving my job, friends and roots.

My parents had died two years earlier. I was glad to have spared them the pain of yet another divorce in their family: out of five children—four daughters and four divorces.

We've often commented that having alcoholic parents was not just coincidental to our lack of successful relationships. But we were gratified that my parents were eventually dry and became faithful members of Alcoholics Anonymous for the last seven years of their lives. Perhaps my siblings and I just weren't good in relationships for lots of other reasons. Besides, I've been told that the statute of limitations for blaming your parents runs out when you reach age 40!

I gathered what possessions I felt I could claim and put them into storage and slid into the car, not really knowing which direction to take. Although I had had six interviews for teaching jobs from Seattle to San Francisco, none had come to fruition.

In retrospect, I'm sure that my cry for a little rest and relaxation virtually screamed to the interviewers that I was the classic burned-out teacher badly in need of time off. If I didn't know it, the interviewers certainly did. My heart just was not into teaching again, at least right away, but I had no other profession. And I had nowhere to go, geographically or otherwise.

From Washington there was no point in heading west; I would bump into the Pacific Ocean in short order. I considered Oregon, but memories of living on the Oregon coast for my first year of teaching after college brought shivered memories of mildew from constant rain seeping into my pores. Efforts at finding a place to live in the high desert of Bend, Oregon, left me empty-handed. Farther to the south was California—earthquakes, Valley Girls, and way too many people. No appeal there!

The choice then was going east or north. At the last minute I called a college that was advertising a canoe trip in British Columbia. Only a couple of hundred dollars would buy use of a canoe, food, guiding, and five college credits—useful if I wanted to maintain my teaching certificate. I got in touch with the couple organizing the trip and convinced them I was in no need of the all day pre-trip meeting, which I'd already missed. Because of a last minute cancellation, I wormed my way into the group.

So north it would be, at least for the first month, away from my home of fifteen years. I had a couple of weeks before the ten-day canoe trip began on the Bowran Lakes.

I detoured to the San Juan Islands in the northwest region of Washington and enjoyed the Fourth of July on a beach with Mt. Baker shining from across the water. I suddenly felt good. There was hope for the future.

The canoe trip on a series of lakes less than a hundred miles south of Prince George was a godsend. Paddling out my frustrations that had built up over the last decade, I soaked up a rare British Columbia sun and let my mind rest. For a brief respite, I didn't trouble myself with any of life's heavy, traumatic decisions, such as where I was going to live or what I was going to do for money.

> I was being cleansed by the adventure, enjoying every moment of it.

We were canoeing in beautiful scenery with nothing to worry about. Except for one day, bad weather and waves never materialized. And we saw only one bear come into camp that managed to mangle a polyethylene water bottle before we yelled and frightened him away. I was being cleansed by the adventure, enjoying every moment of it. By the time the trip ended, I was ready to try the world again on my terms.

I had convinced my brother that, for a few weeks during the summer, Canada might be a welcome relief from 98°F. muggy Los Angeles where he was living. He arranged to fly to Prince George where I would meet him after my canoe trip.

My brother, you have to understand, is a unique individual. Not only does he have a Ph.D. in psychology from University of California at Berkeley, he also was an excellent gymnast and just missed being a member of the 1960 Olympic team. Given all his talents, he has chosen to own and operate a used record and bookstore in South Lake Tahoe. He enjoys his life, and I can only admire his determined choice of the laid-back record business over the high-powered life in psychology.

We planned to drive around British Columbia and Alberta for a few weeks with no real destination. However, we did have to come to a few understandings during our trip. We both wanted to spend some time in Jasper and Banff National Parks. A little hiking and kicked-back touring was the idea. However, he insisted that since one of his objectives of the trip was to buy used records for his store, we had to allow time to stop at antique stores so that he could peruse the possible merchandise for his shop.

The agreement was that only two such stops a day were permitted since looking through records was not high on my list of things to do. Thankfully, he had already scoured Prince George when I arrived. But we made one last stop for an old record player so he could play the 78-rpm records he bought. Forget the fact that he already had one player with him; this one was better, along with the two more he eventually bought along the way. And somehow he fit them all in his suitcase! I wondered if he actually had brought any change of clothes.

We drove south through Sun Valley, Idaho, a place where I considered settling. The beauty of the valley is undeniable. I decided rather quickly that the remoteness and one-industry mindset—even if it is skiing—wasn't what I needed in my life at that time.

After a few days of soaking up the sun, we drove on and decided to visit our cousin in Boulder, Colorado, where my brother departed by train back to Los Angeles after buying more records, and, God knows, maybe another record player!

My cousin, who had lived in Boulder for many years, had been as close as a brother at one time, but over the years we had fallen out of touch. Now maybe we could renew those ties. Why not? I weighed the options, and with a sigh and a sense of resignation, I decided that Boulder seemed to be a good place to live, at least for awhile. I had attended college in Colorado Springs, had always liked Colorado, and had returned to the state for various ski vacations.

I found a decent condominium to rent, and, to my dismay, realized that Boulder was not one of the cheaper places to live. I wasn't sure how I would manage the financial side of such a move but trusted something would work out. I couldn't move in for another month, so I toured Colorado, visiting old friends and camping out a lot. I spent a free week in Steamboat Springs at a condo advertised as a promotional gimmick. The mountain bike rides up to the natural hot springs helped ease the pain of the traumatic change in my life. But, now that I had a place to live, what would I do? I wasn't quite "settled in" with my new life yet.

By September, I was able to move into my own condo; my belongings arrived a week later. Boulder was a new world for someone who had spent the last fourteen years in an out-of-the-way town of five hundred loggers and farmers. I had been raised in a well-to-do suburb of Chicago and was no stranger to the cultured life. But it had been a long time since I'd been in a location where I could easily drive to classes in any given subject. And they were only minutes away, not the hour or two on bad roads I had experienced in Washington. Movies were down the street; stores were close at hand. I felt like a kid in a candy store. There was a recreation center less than a mile away complete with pool, gym and choice of fitness classes.

I was determined to take advantage of as much as possible. Who knew where I'd be next year (Little did I know I would still be in Boulder 15 years later!) Too many years had been spent in a valley closing in on me for five winter months, with only one store, one bar and one restaurant connected to the gas station in town for excitement.

I walked through town feeling like a hayseed in the big city. I strained to soak up all the diverse opportunities Boulder offered. Home to the right wing *Soldier of Fortune* magazine at one time, a major American Buddhist center, a city block full of lounging '60s hippies, more Liberals per square mile than many places in the country, Boulder certainly offered a variety of experiences. However, I found life is much easier for you in Boulder if you are a Liberal. Boulder prides itself in accepting diversity, but God help you if you show diversity of political opinion!

Known as Tofu Town, the People's Republic of Boulder, "Ten Square Miles Surrounded by Reality," and other such appellations, Boulder, in fact, is fun. I eventually took a woodworking class but quickly discovered I shouldn't be in the same room with machines that eat fingers for snacks. I also signed up for lessons in Aikido and the Japanese language.

By December I was working as a sales clerk at an outdoor sports store, substitute teaching in the Boulder Valley School District, and taking classes to become a paralegal. Then I saw an ad in the University of Colorado campus newspaper, which I couldn't resist. The Continuing Education program was offering a class in Highland bagpiping! I had always wanted to learn to play the bagpipes. Some of these other things had to go, but a future learning the bagpipes wasn't one of them.

Taking a bagpipe class was a life-changing decision. I fulfilled an aspiration long thought out of reach. Now, in my late 30s, I was in a situation where I could actually tackle the crazy instrument that had been calling to me for so many years.

I signed up for the class and was soon swept up into a brave new world. The bagpipe class led me to places I had never dreamed of seeing physically and mentally. I dropped woodworking, Aikido, Japanese language in return for bagpiping and a class in teaching gifted and talented students.

I also got thoroughly wrapped up in a fitness class at the recreation center after I saw the participants running up and down the stairs, laughing and perspiring at the same time. Thirty years later I am still attending the same class and have developed wonderful friendships.

Only a few months after leaving Washington, I had found myself in a totally new environment, enjoying my new freedom. Boulder had been a good choice after all. When I wasn't substitute teaching, working at the sports store or taking classes, I was practicing my chanter, the recorder-like instrument which teaches you bagpipe fingering. I was learning how to play tunes in anticipation of playing them on my pipes. That summer I even ventured to Coeur d'Alene, Idaho, for a two-week bagpiping school!

So, why do I play the pipes? I've been waiting for some cantankerous old lady to ask me that question someday. "Well, lady, who wouldn't want to play something that, with three drones, a chanter, and a blowstick, has five phallic symbols?"

3

BRIGADOON IN IDAHO

Piping is serious, and people were there both to improve their playing and help others. The intensity was strong but the magic of the atmosphere kept the outside world at bay.

A bagpiping school in Coeur d'Alene, Idaho? If there is truly a real Brigadoon, a magical place protected from the outside world that appears once in a hundred years, the school in Coeur d'Alene came close. But the school went one better by occurring once every year. More than a hundred pipers from across the U.S. and Canada gathered on the shores of spectacular 25-mile-long Lake Coeur d'Alene on the North Idaho College campus and lived in another world for two weeks.

Started in the late 1960s by Lt. Col. John McEwing who was stationed nearby in the U.S. Air Force, the school developed through the years as a haven for learning the pipes. Attracting some of the best pipe instructors from Scotland such as the one-of-a-kind Evan McCrae and the world-renowned Andrew Wright, this school was a gold mine for someone like me trying to immerse myself in the formidable challenges of playing bagpipes.

Classes began at 8 a.m. and continued until 4 p.m. with an hour lunch break. Students had an hour before dinner to carouse with beers before dinner at 5, then a quick self-practice until 7, recitals by instructors until 8:30 p.m., more practice until, finally, at about 9:30 p.m., a steady stream of worn-out, weary pipers would slip over to the Fort Ground Tavern two blocks away.

Camaraderie and conversation about pipes was always aided by liberal amounts of beer. After midnight, we would slowly maneuver ourselves back to the dorms to recover for the next day's equally demanding tasks. Sleep was not high on the priority list of things to do.

All day long pipes were being played somewhere, much to the chagrin of neighbors who worked night shifts.

Some twelve different classes separated into levels of ability were spread out into various classrooms. Time was divided between chanter practice, practicum, and actual pipe practice conducted outside.

Fortunately for the neighbors, not all the classes practiced outside at the same time. Even at that, some confrontations added excitement to the students' lives. Had the residents ever liked bagpipes, year after year of hearing beginners squeak and squawk can deaden even the heartiest of pipe lovers. One day, the nearby auto mechanics class had had enough and stormed out of their garage, wielding wrenches and other intimidating tools of the trade.

Pipers are generally sensitive to listeners' wishes. If asked to play elsewhere, they usually don't hesitate to comply. But the mechanics-to-be were not in the mood to make polite requests. In response, several pipers were ready to go to battle stations. But $1,000-$3,000 instruments don't make good hand-to-hand weapons, and the pipers exercised discretion and slowly backed away. Not surprisingly, word came down from the administration the next day to avoid the area around the garage in the future.

Such logistical class problems notwithstanding, the school was one of the highlights of my early years of learning bagpipes. There were students and instructors who returned year after year. I attended for five consecutive years. Eight-year veterans were not uncommon. Regular 50-weeks-a-year workaholics used their only two-week vacation to become better pipers.

Instant empathy and rapport developed among the students. Fourteen-year-olds helped the 43-year-old strugglers, and the 57-year-old helped the newer pipers. Piping is serious, and people were there both to improve their playing and help others. The intensity was strong but the magic of the atmosphere kept the outside world at bay. International disasters, bosses, financial problems, all faded into insignificance. There were just bagpipes, music, and the magic of the moment.

Pipers come in all sizes and with their own idiosyncrasies. One instructor wanted to see how long he could go without sleep during the two weeks! Another instructor never did sober up for the duration of the school, but his fingers were like lightning, and he could play more zippy jigs than I knew existed.

During the second week there is always a jig and hornpipe competition and costumes are encouraged. One year we put an instructor in a woman's bathing suit. He liked it so much he left it on after the contest for the rest of the evening! As a friend and I dressed up another well-liked instructor in a silk dress, blond wig and make-up, we added the special touch of earrings made out of bagpipe drone reeds. He stuffed pillows up front for boobs and a big one in back for a cushy rear end. Pipes are difficult enough to play without such accoutrements, but he rose to the occasion and added a cute wiggle to the pillows as he played. The crowd roared with approval. Sometimes, even a Ninja turtle would appear.

One year, this same instructor toasted the judge by drinking a can of bag seasoning—a repulsive-smelling concoction, which is used to keep the leather bag supple and prevents air leaks. This so took us by surprise that we all felt a wave of nausea.

The ingredients are not listed on the can. The best guess is soap—glycerin and anhydrous lanolin with a binder and probably something like Dettol to prevent mold growth. No one had ever thought that this stuff would be drinkable except for this particular piper. The story of this incident spread throughout the bagpipe world within weeks. Those who knew the piper were not totally surprised.

The contest saw instructors competing against other instructors and against the best students. Jigs and hornpipes are perhaps the biggest crowd pleasers because

Alan Walters is in drag for the Jig and Hornpipe Contest.

of their quick, lively tempos. The otherwise run-down, undistinguished, hole-in-a-wall tavern became packed. The students crowded in along with locals who had become camp followers. Piper after piper in costumes ranging from pigs to women to bees to Santa Claus to practically nothing but underwear played their best. Prizes were awarded and the party continued into the night.

One year I witnessed a sight that had rarely been seen before but is now commonplace. After the crowd cleared out from the contest, one of the drumming instructors brought out his drum trap set. Another drummer and piper tuned up their electric guitars. A piper jumped in and an unusual jam session was born. The combination worked! The musicality among the players was demonstrated from the start. The piper might have started with a jig and the drums and guitars would follow, each complementing the other. One of the players might then play some hornpipes and the rest would join in with the variations.

Even after two and a half hours, at three in the morning, I was still yelling for more. Of course, the idea caught on and now there are many bands out there complete with pipes, guitars, trap set, etc., playing any kind of music there is. But I'd like to think I observed the forefront of the movement.

And, sure enough, several days later the group set up instruments in the lobby of one of the dorms. As I returned from class one afternoon, I heard the soul-moving sounds and grabbed my tape recorder. This was before the time of smart phones. I peered over the numerous heads in the gathering crowd to see the piper stripped down to his shorts blowing heartily into the bag.

The drums and guitars were getting the feel of the mood, and everyone was transported to another world. It was absolute bliss!

All of a sudden, the 11-year-old son of one of the instructors joined in with his pipes. He started in without missing a beat. They all played even more jigs and never slowed a bit. The kid was incredible! He not only kept up with them, he started giving them hand signals on what to play next. And it turned out he was actually a better drummer than piper! Scary to think of what he would be like in ten years.

The two lead instructors came directly from Scotland. Both Evan McCrae and Andrew Wright were well known and respected pipers the world over. They couldn't be paid what they were worth, but they came anyway because of the wonderful, friendly atmosphere of the school. Evan was the old ex-military pipe major who, in later years, devoted more time to teaching than playing and was a first-class gentleman. Andrew, incredibly, had memorized all of the piobaireachd literature (pronounced "pee-broch").

Piobaireachds are the classical music of bagpipes and are the earliest form of bagpipe music. Some may have been written more than 600 years ago! Piobaireachds contain a theme or "ground." This theme is repeated in many variations with increasing difficulties for fingers. These pieces can go on for 15-20 minutes or more and must be played from memory. There are, at last count, some 150 piobaireachds!

I fell in love with this particular type of music, but not everybody becomes enamored by piobaireachds. A fellow piper frequently went out of his way to say he would rather eat broken glass than listen to a piobaireachd. This ceol mor, or "big music" as it is formally called, is, at the very least, incredibly mesmerizing ... it's just not to everybody's taste.

Evan and Andrew were also just very nice people who would go out of their way to pay attention to struggling pipers like myself. But a problem arose when I tried communicating with Andrew. He had such a strong Scottish brogue that I had a hard time translating what he said. In fact, there were times that I would lose an entire sentence or even a paragraph. After one such conversation where he spent a good five minutes explaining something to me, he noticed my dazed look. "Ya dint understand one word of what I said, did ye?" I had to confess that, no, indeed, I had not caught even one word!

On the other hand, he delighted in what he called my accent. After our first meeting, he remarked that I must have come from a different area than most of the students at the school. Since most were from the Northwest and Canada, I had to admit that my roots were in the Midwest—Chicago and Wisconsin. Somehow he could discern the difference in my words and would toyfully kid me about *my* accent. I was quite amused when he did this in his strong Scottish brogue.

The school would go to some lengths to promote public relations for its Scottish Studies program. The school session, for a few years, would coincide with the Fourth of July. And Coeur d'Alene put on quite a parade to mark the occasion. The locals marched down their main street for what seemed like hours. The crowd loved it.

As a gesture of good will, all one hundred pipers and drummers of the school would take time off from classes and form up on the other side of town. Without so much as a cursory tuning, we played "Scotland the Brave" and "Green Hills of Tyrol" some twenty times each. These tunes are so familiar that pipers can play them in their sleep. To make it more interesting, some pipers reversed the top and bottom hands on the chanter—very difficult indeed!

The sight and sound of so many pipers is nothing but awesome. The sound is so strong and powerful, the lack of tuning is unimportant. Watching the crowd as we approached was uplifting. Because they had been numbed by all the entries up to that point—the fire engines, costumed dogs, and endless Girl Scout troops—the crowd had become weary.

As the band approached, though, feet started tapping, eyes lit up, and people started to applaud with enthusiasm. One year, after waiting for more than an hour for our spot in the parade to pass so we could play in our order, we decided we really had to get back to our classes. So, we slid right in front of some unsuspecting group. Some enterprising piper wrote a tune about the band that "interrupted" the parade.

The Coeur d'Alene Bagpipe School has undergone many mutations and experienced numerous growing pains since the early 1990s. One year all the classes had to take place outdoors because the classrooms were being renovated. Then the dorms were torn down and housing became challenging for a year. The clientele has changed through the years, and old-timers like me don't attend as much. There are other bagpipe schools, to be sure, but my five consecutive summers going to Coeur d'Alene was a definite "change of life" experience. Sadly, I heard that the school has recently closed its doors.

4
CRISSCROSSING
CHINA

I asked our leader, George: "Do you think it would be
okay if I brought a musical instrument on the trip?"

"Sure ... as long as it isn't ... ha ... ha ... a cello."

"Well, you may be wishing that it was. I play
the bagpipes."

There was a long pause, then a sputtered guffaw,
"...the bagpipes?"

I was thriving in Boulder and working as a substitute teacher. I was also working as a sales clerk in a sports store, a job that, even though described as part-time and temporary, lasted five years. I was immersed in learning bagpipes and enjoying the incomparable experiences of belonging to a bagpipe band. But as spring of the following year approached, I found myself reaching out for something new. I wanted to take advantage of my new situation—no permanent job, no mate to consider, no pets or kids to take care of. I didn't even have any plants to water! Lots of travel brochures crossed my desk.

I began to seriously contemplate a different kind of venture. One of my friends was planning to go to the Beijing Institute of Languages in China for part of the summer. This sounded intriguing. As I researched the possibility of going, I felt like I wanted to see more of China than just Beijing. Because many travel companies are started by somebody who just wants to travel for free, the wise traveler proceeds with caution and reads brochures very carefully and critically compares the various options.

After what I considered to be due deliberation, I decided on an organization that combined biking and touring. The combination of difficulties of organizing a trip where I would be traveling alone, along with the language and logistical problems of a country like China convinced me that I would have to swallow some pride (I liked being on my own) and sign up with a group. Traveling alone has some advantages, but the overwhelming drawback is that you're not able to share experiences with someone close. Even if such a situation can offer incentives to meet interesting people, I chose to travel with a group for this trip.

The move to Boulder had been so successful that I wanted to continue to fully experience my new freedom and to develop the path of discovery that I was on. As long as I was going to check out China, I felt I might as well explore Japan too. I had the time, some money, and the desire and need to open up my life after a fourteen-year marriage and life in the backwoods.

The trip to China concluded in Hong Kong. Five days later, a three-week hiking trek was scheduled to commence in Japan with yet another adventure travel outfit. I had given up looking for some other soul with time and money who was also looking for unusual experiences.

I had learned a long time ago that waiting for such people to commit to travel only decreased your own chances of making the trip. I would decide to make the trip… if someone joined me, fine. If not, I would charge ahead anyway. I was going to China and Japan and would return two months later. I would go with or without a companion.

Although I was an experienced traveler, I did little preparation for my trip to China. I spent the previous weeks before departure moving out of my condominium and putting things in storage. I would be traveling for more than two months and, when I returned, I had arranged to spend another two to three months house-sitting for a friend. All this warranted moving out of my expensive digs to save money.

Since I was taking the easy route of travel by going with an organized group, I decided to take advantage of all the tour company's preparation. I simply wouldn't do any. Having taken some courses in Chinese history and culture through the years, I had not attended to the itinerary ... or much else, for that matter. I had had enough to do upending my life and moving things back into storage again after only two years in Boulder.

I had spoken on the telephone with George, the trip leader. As we were bantering away, the thought of bringing my bagpipes along occurred to me. I didn't realize the potential ramifications of it all at the time. I was primarily concerned about maintaining a practice schedule of some sort. I didn't want to lose my "lip," and I wanted to maintain and even increase my ability at what fingering technique I had learned so far. I also thought mixing Scottish and Chinese cultures could be interesting.

I had been taking lessons for two years by now. The first nine months had been devoted to learning the complicated and awkward fingering on the practice chanter. I had started to actually blow into the pipes a little more than a year before I was to leave for China. I was enjoying the frustrations and joys of the beast and thought I was beginning to sound presentable—a common beginner's mistake. The axiom in the piping world, however, is that it takes seven years and seven generations to really learn bagpiping. I was nowhere close to the seven years predicted for a bagpiper to become proficient. But then again, what would the Chinese know about bagpipes?

I asked our leader, George: "Do you think it would be okay if I brought a musical instrument on the trip?"

"Sure … as long as it isn't—ha—ha— a cello."

"Well, you may be wishing that it was. I play the bagpipes."

There was a long pause, a sputtered guffaw, and "… the bagpipes?"

"Yes, I think I can fit them in my daypack. I won't play them at 6 a.m. or past midnight. Would the Chinese ever want to confiscate them?"

"Uh—no—I don't suppose so. Yeah, bring them along. It certainly would be different."

So, it was decided. My bagpipes would accompany me to the Far East. I hadn't checked with the leader of the Japan hike, but that could be addressed later. I hadn't even figured out what I would do with them in Japan. For now, I gathered my clothes into a convertible travel pack and my pipes in a daypack. The long drones can be dismantled into smaller sections. So, on a warm August day, I settled myself on the plane to Beijing.

A two-hour layover in Los Angeles turned into a seven-hour delay due to one of those famous plane malfunctions that mean anything from an absent crew member to the plane about to fall apart. We weaseled our way onto business class when departure time did arrive. I settled into the unaccustomed luxury of free drinks and room to move without jamming an elbow into the rib of a seatmate.

The delay in L.A. meant that, of course, upon arrival in Tokyo, we discovered we had missed our connecting flight to Beijing. Just as we started to resign ourselves to spending the night at an airport hotel, we were shuffled off in the direction of a People's Republic of China (PRC) Airline's flight to Beijing.

Hustling down back stairways, through unnamed doors and enduring an extra luggage and body check —this was long before the extra delays caused by 9/11— only

increased my apprehension of a bagpipe confiscation.
Apparently, airport personnel have seen stranger things,
and my bagpipes proceeded with me without comment.
We finally sank into one of PRC's cramped, alcohol-free
planes, somewhat rumpled but relieved to be en route.

My grogginess was not severe enough to ignore the piped-in music in the plane. Was I really

> Was I really hearing "My Cheatin' Heart" on one of Communist China's airplanes?

hearing "My Cheatin' Heart" on one of Communist
China's airplanes? I slept through the two-hour
propaganda in-flight film highlighting China's top tourist
sites, including a full hour of acrobatics the Chinese love
so much. The incongruity of this music to the video
foreshadowed the complexity of 1987 China. Remember,
this was before the Tiananmen Square massacre of 1989.

I feel fortunate that I was able to see China before the
big bang of China's economy and change of pace. I could
appreciate the absence of too many cars as well as the
absence of unbreathable pollution of "modern" China.
I felt I was in a country that predated present-day U.S.
by 100 years or more. So much work was done by hand,
including major roadwork. Old hand-run rock-crushing
machines and people smashing big rocks with heavy
hammers were de rigeur.

I've been told a major transformation of a country from the 19th century into the 21st century took about 30 years, as soon as the Chinese government loosened its grip on how businesses were operated. Exemplifying this change is the story of a woman who was barely able to afford a moped to take her child to school in 1995. In 2005, that child, now 22, bought an Infiniti!

Twenty-eight hours after leaving Denver, about 2:00 a.m. China time, I unwisely took two sleeping pills in our Beijing hotel. I had never used sleeping pills before and had been cautioned to test them beforehand. That had been one of the warnings I had not read in the rush to pack. I quickly discovered that one pill—maybe even half a pill—would have been more than sufficient rather than the two I gulped down. Unfortunately, I hadn't calculated that we would be awakened after only three hours of sleep.

We were roused for our first bike ride early in the morning, Chinese-time. Stumbling to the welcome shower, I hazily noticed that the showerhead had to be hand-held. What I didn't fully appreciate was the total lack of any shower curtain. In a state resembling a drunken stupor, I thoroughly enjoyed the cleansing water, showering merrily, not paying attention to

where the showerhead pointed. This had the effect
of leaving pure devastation for my 57-year-old
roommate. She had to wonder what kind of a person
would drench an entire bathroom in less than three
minutes. Shortly, she would wish that that had been
my only quirk.

Actually, she came to find relief in my idiosyncrasies
compared to those of our fellow travelers. Our group
was relatively small, just ten of us including the leader.
The group had the requisite bad apple and an older
gentleman who was a self-proclaimed authority on
everything. It also included a quiet, introspective
doctor-to-be who was preparing for residency, two
naïve, neophyte younger women travelers, and a
motley assortment of others.

The bad apple and his young wife were completing
a world tour for their honeymoon. Obviously China
had been her choice; The Canary Islands had been
his. His goal was to make sure she knew he was just
appeasing her by agreeing to stop in China. There was
no way he was going to allow himself to have a good
time. He remained sitting in the bus, head in a book,
refusing not only to get out, but also even to look
or listen to the impressive cacophony of sounds and
sights of a fascinating farmers' market in rural China.

Sadly, the only thing to make him happy would be if everyone else in the group became grumpy as well.

My roommate, on the other hand, enjoyed everything in sight and never seemed to be bothered by her "advanced" age of 57, which now, with a different perspective, seems quite young. The seventy-year-old "authority" did have a saving grace. Harold had the foresight to bring balloons to pass out to all the kids who magically appeared in the various towns we rode through. Without the balloons this delightful portion of the population may never have emerged, and we would have missed a wonderful opportunity to mingle with the locals.

The two gals in their early thirties seemed interesting and nice enough at the beginning. But what had started out as good company soured after George, our tour leader, spent more time with me than the two of them. Meanwhile, George's friend from architectural school, Bill, seemed to enjoy spending a lot of time with our Chinese interpreter, who, ironically, many years later, married our tour leader! The "doc" escaped into himself, and most of my fellow travelers had nothing of interest to provide on the trip. Fortunately, they didn't have to as China provided plenty of mind-boggling sights.

5

A START IN BEIJING

As I struck up the first few notes, several workers in the vicinity immediately halted their work. I learned quickly just how curious and direct the Chinese are. No sideways glances and polite distances here. The Chinese apparently approach curiosities directly and unabashedly. And, I must admit, I was a curiosity.

The sights, sounds and smells that met me on our first bike ride were overwhelming. The smell was dusty and musty with a hint of spicy food being cooked and wafting in the atmosphere. Beijing had wide boulevards even then, but eerily not much traffic; much of the population was unable to afford cars at that time. My head was on a continual pivot as we started out into the streets of Beijing toward the Summer Palace, only a few miles away. Perhaps it was the infusion of strange and curious sights that distracted me. Perhaps it was just confusion. Three of us immediately proceeded to get separated from the group—within the first block—and were lost.

Our interpreter, a necessary and required accoutrement for a tour group, according to the Chinese government at that time, worked for the Beijing Sports Service, one of the tourist organizations that oversaw foreigners. She led the core of the group off in the proper direction, while George and I waited for seventy-year-old Harold who had fallen off his bike and skidded on the pavement.

When we three gathered ourselves up again, the rest were nowhere to be seen. George took off in what he thought was the correct way to the palace. After a mile or so, we reversed our direction 180 degrees and somehow eventually arrived at the correct meeting spot, not too far behind the others.

I managed to get lost twice that day! The first time with George hardly counted. Not so the next time. An hour later, I found myself lost again. This time I was alone. Extensive and architecturally fascinating, the Summer Palace is comprised of many lakes, gardens and palaces. Longevity Hill and Kunming Lake dominate the expansive park-like area.

As we slowly roamed the palace grounds in an amoeba-shaped, slow-moving group, I ventured a few steps away from the group to take the proverbial quick photo of this lovely lake. Sure enough, when I turned around, all I saw were Chinese faces. Not a Caucasian to be seen anywhere. My group had disappeared. It was the lake's fault!

It was a large crowd, as expected in China, but nary a one was non-Chinese. I wandered in the same direction the group had been headed, not too concerned yet. I didn't catch up with them as I figured I would. I kept walking, assuming I would see them eventually. Finally, with a twitch of nervousness settling in the pit of my stomach, I concluded that I had missed a turn ... or two.

Here I was, my first day in China, in a crowd of Chinese, and me without a word of Chinese or any idea of where I was. George had vaguely mentioned something about meeting at the North Gate for the bus ride back to our hotel. I found out quickly that very few Chinese spoke English. "North Gate" meant nothing. I garbled *bei mens* or something like that, a phrase I'd barely caught from Xiao Fan, our young, lovely interpreter, that meant

"North Gate," but I was met with blank stares. I kept walking, kept asking, and started to be a bit concerned that I'd spend the rest of my days in the Summer Palace.

Finally someone seemed to understand my Chinese utterance and pointed in the direction I was headed. Now I started to jog, oblivious of the sight that an American running in tight bike shorts must have presented to the locals. Had I had the foresight to bring my bagpipes with me, I could have used them as a locating beacon for my group to find me. Alas, I had left the bike with the tour organizers and my bagpipes in the hotel. I would bring the pipes along with me regularly after that day.

I arrived at the bus just as the others did but from another direction. I had survived. Since I eventually had found my group in time, my confidence ballooned. The resulting sense of self-assurance would help me throughout the trip. No more would I worry about finding myself alone. In fact, I sought opportunities to have some time away from the group. Walking the streets by myself or with just one or two others proved to be one of the greater joys of discovering China. And ... I would get lost again.

This I did the very next evening. A nearby park lured me to its paths, which led to back streets. I appreciated the Chinese taking advantage of some spare time by boating on the lake in the park with their now-abbreviated families. China had instituted the one child per family rule to curb its overpopulation. Only just recently has the Chinese government decided to allow all married couples to have two children.

I also contemplated the dichotomy of the community television brought into the courtyard on a crate from a corrugated aluminum home with a dirt floor. I understand things have changed dramatically since 1987 when I visited. The Chinese in 2015 claim to have 325 televisions for every 1,000 people, though I have learned to question statistics from the Chinese government. I was struck by the friendliness of the crowd surrounding the television. Many offered a chair for me to sit on and watch with them.

In 1987, few cars were seen but bikes were everywhere, though they were the clunky, one speed, hard-seat model. Only a few years later, China would be the major producer of mountain bikes exported to the United States. But we drew crowds whenever we stopped in dirt road towns. People gathered to marvel at our eight speed gears.

Moreover, manual labor was the prevailing approach to getting things done. In fact, in the next four weeks, I saw little machinery. Everything was done by brute force.

Chinese were intrigued with our many gears in 1987.

Road-building crews moved huge house-size boulders by hand. I wondered what all these laborers would do if machines replaced them? China is currently discovering this. Their leap into the 21st century has startled the world, as well as themselves.

That afternoon after the visit to the palace, I attempted my first outside bagpipe practice, around the nearest corner from the hotel. I had several purposes for bringing the pipes: for needed practice time; a useful tool to help me mix with the populace; and as an exercise in fusing disparate cultures.

Set off on a side street away from the mainstream, our hotel was in a relatively quiet part of Beijing. My practice, on a semi-sidewalk, surrounded by a lot of junk haphazardly strewn about, the spot was observable only from a small brick factory across the street from where I stood. Few people were near.

As I struck up the first few notes, several workers in the vicinity immediately halted their work. I learned quickly just how curious and direct the Chinese are. No sideways glances and polite distances here. The Chinese apparently approach curiosities directly and unabashedly. And, I must admit, I was a curiosity.

These workers moved in close and stared straight at me. I played for a half hour or so, and the workers listened for the entire time without so much as a twitch. I can only imagine what such a work stoppage would cause in America's heavy work-ethic society. But, here in China, I don't doubt that even the boss of the brick company was one of the listeners.

Without an interpreter, I could only assume that their questions after I stopped playing pertained to my bagpipes. Doubting that a Chinese word existed specifically for "Scottish Highland bagpipes," I told them the English word, and that was about the extent of our verbal communication. Trying to interact in a more meaningful way went nowhere, and, glumly, they returned to work, and I later reported my encounter to my group.

I realized that any further interaction I would have with the Chinese would be limited without a translator. In the future, if I wanted to get the most out of my mixing with the locals, I would need George with his limited but adequate Chinese, or our official translator, Xiao Fan. Otherwise the Chinese and I were stuck with hand signals and grunts, a most unsatisfactory way to communicate.

I love an adventure and quickly realized that here was a chance to interact with the locals on a different level. I was in a position to be instrumental, literally, in a juxtaposition of cultures. How does an American, playing the Scottish bagpipes, interact with the different ethnicities of the Chinese? Can music be an impetus to bring different cultures together? Or would the weird music push the two cultures apart? Or is it true that music is the real "international language?" I would find out in the weeks to come, and in years to come in other countries.

Splashes of color contrasting with the drab concrete structures all around surrounded me. Post Cultural Revolution, pre-Tiananmen Square Massacre days saw an increased awareness of Western approaches to life. The women were wearing dresses that could almost be called stylish, if not colorful. The Mao suits, named for Mao Zedong, the Communist leader of China, had been popular and almost required in the 1960s. Now they were noticed only because there were so few of them. I marveled at the contraptions women used for hair permanents. The convoluted, torturous gizmos they wore on their heads dated from the American twenties. But the fact that Chinese women were getting permanents at all signified a change from Mao days.

Still, most things in 1987 seemed to date back to the way things were almost a century ago in the United States. In fact, in the 25 years since I made my visit, a new world has opened up in China, due, apparently, to an initial embracing of the capitalistic system. I was fortunate enough to be able to see the beginning of this conversion.

I started to relax after a few days. Jet lag was wearing off and my eyes were returning to normal after an initial sensory overload. It was an effort to adjust to the still-hot boiled water left in a carafe on the nightstand for our safe drinking water. The water was invariably still warm the next morning and not very desirable for quenching thirst. Sights and smells competed with the continuous sounds of another world.

My first taste of rural China came the next morning. Awakened at 3 a.m., we planned to arrive at the Great Wall at sunrise. Due to light traffic at that hour, we arrived in a little more than an hour instead of the usual two needed during normal traffic hours. Eating our boxed breakfast in the bus, not a sound could be heard. Slowly, the mist and fog surrounding us became more and more dense. The outline of the Great Wall was barely discernible less than 100 yards away.

It was still dark when, with intense expectation, we approached the famous site. There were no other tourists, or, for that matter, there was nobody in sight. Gingerly feeling our way, we climbed the steps to the top of the wall. Finally, dawn crept its way through the darkness and began to break, but the fog and drizzle settled in for earnest. Any hope of the sun burning through was was wishful thinking.

The swirling clouds lent a magical aura to the edifice and to its long history "hanging in the air" before us. We walked silently by the watchtowers and then restoration improvements became less noticeable and it was more difficult to walk. With growing light, we caught glimpses of the magnitude of the project.

Down through the ages, the wall was built of stone, brick, earth and/or wood to protect the Chinese Empire against its many different invaders. Sections were built at different times and then joined together as time went on. In some places, the wall was so wide that it could handle a chariot with four horses. But, in the end, it was ineffective at stopping the invaders. Nevertheless, the Great Wall of China was built and is one of the great man-made wonders of the world.

The mood was right, the audience sparse, and my courage high. I took out the pipes I had secreted in my daypack. Our group had spread out. I sought out one of the many watchtowers built along the way and started to play. The impact of the sound on those unable to see me was profound and a little spooky. But somehow, in that setting, the music seemed to fit. As mentioned before, the Highland bagpipes are considered a weapon of war, and for good reason. To be heard at the site where Mongol hordes invaded China was eerily appropriate.

I enjoyed playing pipes in the mists of the Great Wall of China.

In fact, perhaps the Chinese would have been more successful had they employed some bagpipes to repulse the Mongols!

The bagpipe scale itself was not as strange to the Chinese as one might think. The Zhou Dynasty, 1046-256 BCE, established a formal system of court and ceremonial music, manifesting the sound of nature integrated into the order of yin and yang. The instruments that were developed correlated to the five elements of nature and used a pentatonic scale. This scale divided an octave into five steps instead of the familiar eight-note scale of Western music. It is perhaps not entirely coincidental that the Highland bagpipe, an instrument designed to play as many pentatonic scales as possible in a limited space and the scales heard in some Chinese music had some tonal similarities.

The mist finally lifted and, as morning progressed, the tourists slowly appeared. The magic of the morning had dissipated along with the mist. I put the pipes away and walked slowly as far as I could in the opposite direction. The wall has only been restored in various sections. Where work stopped, the walk along the top became very hazardous and impossible in some places.

As more and more people crowded onto the scene and the myriads of tour buses arrived, I gave up trying to imagine all the history the wall had witnessed through the hundreds of years. Bagpipes securely tucked away, I retreated and bought the requisite t-shirt at one of the many kiosks. We gathered at the bus to ready our bikes for a welcomed ride through the country.

Fields of corn, roads filled with decrepit three-wheeled tractors, farmers carrying indefinable and perhaps unimaginable foods and other stuffs on carts including a live, strapped-down pig met our eyes. We were greeted with friendly choruses of "hellos" indicating previous contact with English-speaking tourists. As we slowly peddled along we were fascinated by the small, individually owned gardens, the initial Chinese foray into allowing its citizens to determine their own lives.

I can't imagine a better way to acquire the rhythm of a country than to cycle through it.

I would have preferred a longer bike ride that day, but the Ming Tombs were next on our itinerary. A classic tourist trap, Chinese-style, the tombs themselves were rather unimpressive. Perhaps they have "improved" them for the tourists by now. They are simply a collection of imperial mausoleums built by the Chinese Ming Dynasty emperors. I remember a large, mostly empty cavern underground. Perhaps our group was not shown all of the grounds; perhaps the tombs were just something for tourists to say they saw. I was disappointed with what I saw, and our group felt we had been "taken for a ride."

But there are times when tourist sites are well worth seeing, and the Forbidden City is such a place. Expansive and architecturally fascinating, it is a city unto itself. The city is comprised of some 980 buildings; an interested soul could spend weeks poking around its 250 acres. It was the ceremonial and political center of Chinese government for almost 500 years, as well as home to the emperors and their households.

Xiao Fan, our translator and guide, explained that the Red Army had actually seized control of it during the Cultural Revolution when mobs were destroying everything "old" and saved it from almost sure destruction. Sometimes bagpipers actually know when not to play; this was such a time.

We moved on and fought the crowds the next day in Beijing, viewing Mao Zedong's Tomb and visiting various parks, including the zoo. I found myself watching the people instead of the animals, though I succumbed to the famous pandas—as did the Chinese. The Chinese seemed relaxed and totally cognizant of accepting their fate, whatever that might be. While enjoying their small bits of "freedom," they were completely aware that at any given moment another "cultural revolution" could descend upon them without warning.

And perhaps it was that resignation that failed to propel the 1989 Tiananmen Square protest beyond its gory end. Perhaps it was just the tanks and bullets that halted a movement towards freedom. Yet, if nothing else, a visitor sensed the sheer numbers, the jiggling masses of people everywhere, and the potential for greatness as well as disaster.

We flew on to two other areas, Guilin and Kunming, with each jet hop taking us farther into the "outback." At each stop we still contended with people swarming everywhere. Small towns were not as common as I expected. Even smaller places seemed overcrowded due to the fact people were always ... milling. People were walking, riding bikes, bouncing along on the ever-present three-wheeled tractors, and pulling and pushing carts of all sizes and shapes. They never seemed to notice their crowded plight, perhaps unaware that any other condition existed.

6

EXCITEMENT ON THE LI RIVER

To practice tai chi with accompanying bagpipes seemed a startling contrast. Bagpipes are not particularly known for bringing "a state of mental calm and clarity."

Fifteen hundred kilometers to the southwest of Beijing lay Guilin. A very popular tourist area for Chinese and foreigners alike, Guilin offers incredibly unusual geological formations. Many of the scrolls and tapestries sold worldwide depict the Guilin area. Gumdrop-like limestone cones that reach several hundred feet high cover the landscape.

In fact, our airplane approach caused much concern as it seemed as if we would hit at least one of these strange creations. Because Vietnam is only a little more than 300 miles away and known for a hot, humid climate, we should have been prepared for the 95/95 syndrome; that is, 95° F. and 95% humidity. But forewarned or not, I melt in such conditions. Neither biking nor bagpipe playing was the first thing on my mind.

For the first time in my life, I welcomed air-conditioning. It usually feels too cold and artificial for me. We were ensconced in a hotel designed for the foreign tourist. A glassed-in high-rise, it offered the requisite ground floor bar and souvenir shops for the in-and-out tourist. The view from the top, however, was impressive: a 360-degree panorama overlooking the city and surrounding lowlands. I spotted a perfect park across the way, not far from the Li River, to again share my bagpipes with the Chinese once I had recovered from the heat and humidity.

Many Chinese have pet birds of all sizes, colors and shapes, and a common practice throughout much of China is to "air" them in the very early morning hours. They bring their pet birds to the parks and tether them outside their cages. I presume this ritual is as much an opportunity for quiet and peace of mind for the Chinese as it is for the good of the birds. Meanwhile, the early morning also finds various locals practicing tai chi in silent groups.

A Caucasian woman and her blaring bagpipes seemed to me to fit right in! In spite of my reluctance to disturb the tranquility of the morning and as dawn lighted the paths, I found a private tree to pin my music papers to and struck in my pipes. In a matter of minutes, a crowd amassed around me. It seems that the bagpipe sound carries well in the wee hours.

The first person to step out of the crowd was a Western lady with a strong cultured British accent. She had been on the top floor of the hotel waiting for the sunrise when the surprisingly familiar sounds of home drifted to her ears. She had raced down to the street to search out what had to be a compatriot. Although there was a suggestion of disappointment on her face at finding an American woman and not a kinsman playing the pipes, she was clearly appreciative of hearing a touch of home.

I was able to practice one more set of tunes when a Chinese man, who was obviously excited, could wait no longer and began jabbering away in passable English. He was most friendly, and, like most Chinese who know some English, was unrestrained when it came to trying out this strange language. He related how, as a boy, he had been involved with Chennault's Flying Tigers. The Tigers were American World War II pilots who flew over "the hump"— the Himalayas. I wondered if this wasn't something told to all Americans by many Chinese his age, but the truth of his claim was unimportant. He wanted to be friendly, interact, and share words and thoughts with an American.

As it turned out, he was a tai chi master leading the nearby group, and he invited me over to play for them. Tai chi is an ancient form of internal martial art, performed v-e-r-y slowly, with precise, deliberate motions of arms and legs. It is practiced for defense as well as for health benefits. The objective includes focusing the mind on the movements in order to bring a state of mental calm and clarity.

To practice tai chi with accompanying bagpipes seemed a startling contrast. Bagpipes are not particularly known for bringing "a state of mental calm and clarity."

Still, who could resist such an invitation and opportunity? As absurd as the suggestion was, I would not have interacted with the tai chi master had it not been for my bagpipes, and everybody seemed to enjoy the strange juxtaposition. I could see their smiles and feel their laughter.

I returned to the hotel to overhear several gratifying comments from the guests regarding the surprising sound of early morning bagpipes in China. Fortunately, few had wanted to sleep late and everybody seemed to enjoy the sound.

The tai chi master enjoyed moving to the sound of the pipes.
(photo by Dewey Webster)

We biked all over Guilin on its dirt-packed, pot-holed streets—to the Reed Flute Caves, the Seven-Star Park, over questionable bridges, through dust-choked back alleys, and into rush hour. Escaping only by inches from being crushed between bikes and smoke-belching buses, I could only feel complete exhilaration. The gritty dust was unimaginable; the sound of blaring horns and bustling humanity was constant. The Chinese seemed to believe that if a driver actually hit a pedestrian while honking his horn, the driver was in the right.

Aggressive pedestrians and bicyclists were everywhere. The only way to survive was to go with the flow. I was experiencing what the Chinese locals felt every day commuting to work or just going about their daily chores. Perspectives on life have to alter with that life-style. Just what those perspectives were would require more time and insight than I had at that time. I would, however, consider and evaluate those viewpoints for the remainder of the visit. Now it was a challenge just to concentrate on surviving the crush.

We experienced one of the more interesting meals that day. Noonday lunch was never a casual affair. Our hosts, the Beijing Sports Service, believed, not entirely without justification, that good lunches were the way to an American's heart. While it was difficult to find alternatives to their endless supply of watery beer, the food was another story.

I learned quickly not to inquire to closely about what a particular dish was. The best action was just to try it. If it was tasty, I ate it and didn't trouble myself about its origins. I suspect I had eaten snake and dog meat on more than one occasion and, without the sure knowledge of what it was I was eating, found them quite enjoyable.

This day we were served a large middle-of-the-table pot of stew with nameless things floating about. The modus operandi was to fish around with your chopsticks and gather enough on your plate for a taste. As I was weaving my chopsticks back and forth, I finally grabbed onto something substantial. Imagining a firm piece of meat to sink my teeth into, I plucked out an odd looking shape. Peering at it more closely, I made out the distinct eyeballs and beak of a complete chicken's head!

Although I was eager to experience Chinese culture, I wasn't quite ready for chicken beaks and eyeballs. I "accidentally" dropped it back into the pot and fished around some more. This time I came up with a claw-like foot! Undaunted, I let this, too, slip back into the stew, hoping I wasn't starting to appear rude.

I eventually managed to find pieces that were less challenging and enjoyed what was obviously meant to be a special treat. Chicken heads and feet are actually considered the better delicacies to the Chinese. Our guide told me that this lunch included finely chopped pig's stomach with noodles, turtle soup with shells and meat, white fungus soup, vegetable soup, mushrooms with greens, spicy eel with parsnip, and red crayfish. Like I said, sometimes it was better not to ask.

Guilin is a major tourist center, attracting visitors from all over the world, not just to see the famous gumdrop hills but also to travel on the Li River. Floating down the Li affords spectacular views of the karst formations. The river bends and twists like a pig's tail. The tourist boats line up at the dock in a scene vaguely reminiscent of the Dunkirk evacuation, accommodating people clamoring to board from the shore. The sputtering tugboats were of questionable seaworthiness and called to mind reports of "Tourist Boat Sinks; All 200 Lost!" Numbering more than fifteen, the boats gathered up the tiny expectant figures to overflowing capacity and off we charged, mindless of any potential risk.

After several hours of filling my camera full of classic rural scenes and of local fishermen on their four-log rafts, I felt a familiar need welling up inside me. I grabbed my pipes from the cabin and emerged onto the fantail of the boat. Scores of cameras magically appeared before I played the first notes.

I concentrated on the lovely scenery and ignored the cameras, but I couldn't help but notice that the boat immediately behind us closed the distance, and cameras from that boat were enthusiastically clicking away. I played on until lunch was served. Even the Chinese knew their priorities, and those had nothing to do with bagpipes. Food fed the stomach; bagpipe music fed the soul. I stashed my pipes and joined the diners.

Our destination, Yangshuo, was well prepared for the disembarking of tourists ripe for plucking. Most of these consumers would board buses back to Guilin that day

The Li River near Guilin offered inspiration.
(photo by Dewey Webster)

after an hour or two of scooping up whatever geegaws and bric-a-bracs they just had to have. We would stay two nights, giving us a chance to bicycle through the countryside. The hard sell from the hawkers lining the streets was disconcerting and even unwelcome at first.

After being uncharacteristically rude to several persistent merchants, I stepped back from it all and tried to appreciate it from another perspective. Buying, selling, and trading were age-old customs worldwide, certainly in China, dating back to ancient times. The Chinese were only exercising their cultural traditions that had existed long before Mao had mucked things up. And, in 1987, with few economic opportunities available, this buying, selling, trading, and bargaining afforded the Chinese with a critical means to earn money. With this in mind, I started to enjoy the atmosphere and even bought my share of useless goodies among the pottery, woodcarvings and paper maché masks.

George and I inquired about one particular vendor's display of old wooden carved images of all shapes and sizes, which had adorned old doors so prevalent at all the shops. As the conversation progressed, the owner must have sensed a sale. We were taken upstairs in his house and shown his "better" stuff. The furnishings of the house consisted of a bed and … nothing else. There were no dressers, no tables, and no chairs. Otherwise, items for sale littered the floor.

Downstairs, behind the curtain partitioning the sale area from what passed as a "living area," there was a hole in the ground with a faucet. I did not ask to use the bathroom. Many toilet facilities in the smaller towns of China consisted of a toilet house down the street with a narrow pathway on one side and some holes on the other. And it was evident that not everyone bothered to use the holes! I was uncertain as to the cooking facilities, if any, but I didn't ask. In the end, we bought nothing, thanked him for his efforts, and appreciated the opportunity to see "inside" the real China.

The town transformed when the tour buses left. A comparative peace settled over the population, and the buying frenzy abated until the next day and the next boatload of tourists. And as the pace slowed, I detected an increased friendliness from the same entrepreneurs who were hard selling only moments before. I was looking forward to our next day and a half in this lovely spot.

In fact, that night we celebrated my birthday. Surprisingly, another in our small group had the same birthday. As we all prepared for dinner, I burst into Bill's and George's hotel room playing "Happy Birthday" on the pipes. They were duly impressed. I wasn't too sure about the other hotel residents though.

George had arranged a birthday cake, Chinese style. I had detected very little sugar in any Chinese dish, and the cake was no exception. Even if the actual cake itself was not up to standards, the *idea* of a cake was appreciated.

And, in good traditional Chinese fashion, we set off some fireworks later over the river.

That night we boarded another small tourist boat to view night cormorant fishing, an unusual fishing method used in that area. The four-log rafts support a fisherman, basket, bait and six to twelve cormorants, which are long-necked black goose-like birds trained to help the fisherman. With kerosene lanterns glowing to attract the fish, the fisherman poled along, letting the tethered cormorants out onto the water. The birds actually did the fishing. When a bird caught a fish in its long bill, the fisherman hauled the bird in, forcing it to cough up the fish stuck in its throat by a tight collar around its neck. Nifty trick!

The fishing was as fascinating as the Chinese approach to entertaining the tourists on this boat. The boat had chugged over to a backwater area that bred nothing but mosquitoes. As we fought off the unwelcome invaders, a man and a woman on our boat treated us to some singing. I think the mood was supposed to be romantic, but it was too much of a stretch for us. We found it nonsensical and untuneful and were only too happy when the boat moved on and the singing ceased.

We had no trouble entertaining ourselves the next day. We biked to a dingy town called Xingping along the river. We crossed the river into what appeared to be the 18th century.

The town looked like it hadn't changed since its founding. And, with any luck, it wouldn't lose this charm for centuries to come. Narrow cow paths wandered by and seemingly through the huts, which passed for houses. Electricity, television, phones, and all that paraphernalia we can't live without was unknown in this sleepy hamlet in the late 1980s. The inhabitants didn't seem any less satisfied because of the lack of these things. Existence seemed barely tenable here, but still there was a peaceful atmosphere and a slow, patient aura to the place.

Xingping had a few homes and one "restaurant" near the water. Without the guides, I would not have discerned the building as a public eating establishment whatsoever. The label "restaurant" is questionable. Hygiene as we know it is not a Chinese virtue, and I made a mental note to bring my own chopsticks next time.

Our local guide tried to take our minds off the insects crawling on the floor and chickens running in and out by singing American folk songs! "Yankee Doodle" and "Down in the Valley" seemed as much out of place as my bagpipes would have been. But it was certainly better entertainment than the uncertain warbling of the singers the night before.

On our next day's ride, we stopped in various small, dirt-blown towns apparently empty of any life. But when Harold pulled balloons from his pocket and blew them up, children quickly appeared. The road was suddenly filled with these beautiful but dirty faced, curious children who laughed and giggled and greedily snatched the balloons from each other.

Six in the group opted to put their bikes in the bus preferring a bus ride back to town. The remaining three of us split up. For several hours and 15 miles, I had China all to myself.

Pure euphoria took hold of me on my bike ride back to Yangshuo on dirt roads. I waved to Chinese lugging unimaginable loads on their bikes or carts and watched buffalo wallowing in irrigation ditches. I was conscious that I was watching scenes that were replicated in thousands of places in China. I could even enjoy watching the men sitting idly on their haunches on the doorsteps of their houses doing nothing while the women carried 70-pound baskets of goods on their backs.

The slow speed of a bike matched the slowness of life in general. Yet, I was ecstatic to enjoy the experience without listening to all the jabbering from my fellow travelers. Sharing observations is invaluable, but there are times when solo outings offer a different opportunity for reflection.

Women carry the large loads!

Paradoxically, I felt a freedom in a country without much freedom. The soaked rice fields stretched far into the distance until they bumped into the karst formations. Life here emerged day after day at a familiar slow pace. The Chinese seemed to accept their roles and were resigned to their fates or, as they call it, joss.

The Chinese can carry tremendous loads on their bikes, and I realized that riding bikes for sheer pleasure, as we were doing, was not a well-known activity here. I passed one woman whose sun-wracked wrinkled face made her appear to be in her 70s, but she may have been only 50. Her harsh life had aged her. She was carrying a load twice her size and weight. I considered offering to help but was concerned that I would be interfering with the "natural order" of things and, with some guilt, decided to ride on. I was still a foreigner here and, in spite of their friendliness, was unsure as to how such an offer would be received.

With a feeling of full joy upon me after the freshness of my ride, I brought out my pipes when I returned to the hotel. Located at the end of the main street, our hotel was off the road a bit and something between fourth and fifth class lodging. My purpose that day was to practice, not to mix with the population. But, of course, that was nigh impossible in China.

Under some shade trees beside a pond, I struck up "Scotland the Brave." For some reason, the local Chinese here listened from more of a distance than they had in other places. I had room to breathe without bodies pressing in from all sides and intruding on my Western sense of personal space. And I didn't feel so conspicuous either. I actually got some good practice in instead of feeling like I had to perform. That was one of the few times I experienced that situation in all my time in China.

We packed up after lunch and loaded our baggage on the bus. Again, the same three chose to start off on our bikes. As we prepared for our departure, I felt a sudden pain, presumably from lunch. In seconds I realized I needed to return to the hotel room to use the bathroom. We had officially checked out, however. I could not explain the problem well enough to the manager to weasel my way back into my room.

I did manage to find a public bathroom down the hall just in time. But the fourth-class bathroom only had the ubiquitous pit, the standard toilet for the locals. I was happy for anything. To complicate things, I discovered when I left, my aim had been a little off. Using this kind of toilet takes practice. I pitied the poor maid who had to clean up, but the bus driver was honking the horn.

I briefly considered foregoing the bike and riding on the bus until my stomach settled down. But looking at the bus crowd, then the bikes, I sucked in my stomach and grabbed my bike. We would rendezvous with those on the bus in about 14 miles. Yes, they would have to wait awhile for us. I absolutely hate having people wait for me. But this was advertised as a bike trip, and I felt only a little guilty making them wait.

Biking through China's countryside is one of the most relaxing and entertaining adventures I can imagine. Recreation is a little-known concept for the tirelessly working farmers. They looked at us with perhaps as much or more wonder than we did at them.

I was sufficiently recovered by evening to walk about the bustling town of Guilin with its ever-present vendors hawking their wares. George and I bought a bottle of Chinese brandy and rented a rowboat for a tour around the lake across from where we were staying. The liquor was unidentifiably nasty-tasting stuff. It tasted so bad we couldn't finish the bottle, but we drank enough to achieve its purpose and stumbled back to the hotel no longer wondering why we didn't see too many drunk Chinese.

How I felt the next morning was entirely predictable. I was never to feel worse from any of the food I ate in China than I did that morning from the "brandy."

Instead of fighting the nausea, I should have allowed myself to become sick so I could get on with the rest of the day. Instead, I extended the misery.

Our plane had been delayed, and we had several hours to kill. The intern in our group had requested that we visit a Chinese folk hospital; none of the others including myself were interested in seeing a "modern" version of their hospitals. We thought it would be more interesting to see where the masses go. The experience was definitely eye opening.

The smell, or more specifically, the stench of the folk hospital overwhelmed us as soon as we stepped through its entrance. Again, hygiene was not readily apparent. The smell of urine was everywhere. Trying to concentrate on the acupuncture of one patient with 10-inch long needles protruding from her face was not what was needed to quell my growing dizziness. Glass jars suctioned the skin on the back of another fellow.

Following our guide from one room to the next, observing various disagreeable forms of ancient healing, my stomach just wasn't up to the challenge. Increased grumblings and uneasiness precipitated my early departure to the relatively fresh outside. I lay down in our bus and willed my stomach to forget what I had just seen and took a deep breath. When the group went on to lunch, I rested in the bus and managed to feel better upon their return, two hours later.

We were finally ready to leave Guilin and embark on the plane for our journey into the far reaches of southwestern

China to Kunming. Unfortunately, while I was nursing my hangover, George had been frantically searching for the group visa which had disappeared somewhere between the rowboat and the hotel—another unfortunate effect of the Chinese brandy!

The Chinese seem to relish their heavy, slow, and discombobulated bureaucracy. So, the affect of a lost group visa would not be slight. Hoping not to attract too much attention, our group proceeded through the airport security with nonchalance. George had notified our immediate guides of the Beijing Sports Service. They had been madly trying to arrange some interim official form to appease the local authorities.

After passing two checkpoints, we started to breathe easier, but we were stopped at the third and final desk. Panic was evident on the faces of several in our group. They clearly had visions of finding out what the inside of a Chinese jail looked like. After a long delay, several phone calls, and lots of communication involving the police, airport security, George, and our guides, we were passed through. I sensed that the Chinese bureaucrats had enjoyed our discomfort.

7

WEST TO KUNMING

I continued playing until I finally made out the shape of a water buffalo and its master, an old, timeless, slightly bent Chinese man with the classic inscrutable visage. Undaunted, the two of them were not to be denied use of the path, which they, no doubt, had used every day for forty years.

Kunming reaches farther west, almost 500 miles from Guilin in the Yunnan Province. Approaching the Tibetan Plateau, it is higher than Guilin with an elevation of some 6,200 feet and, therefore, mercifully cooler than our previous haunts. Here I could leave the hotel without breaking into a sweat within the first few steps. Driving into town from the airport, eager to see what I hoped would be a smaller town, I quickly discerned a huge city of several hundred thousand people. (In 2015, the population is more than four million.) I was a bit disappointed but was gaining an appreciation for just how populated this country was.

The province entertains at least 21 ethnic minorities, including the Bai, Yi, Naxi, Mosuo, Sani, and, of course, the Han. I had my first encounter with some of these colorful people upon leaving the hotel alone shortly after our arrival. The Sani people are very Tibetan looking; genetic testing has substantiated the relationship between these two groups. Because of their finer and smoother features, there is to me a special beauty to those with Tibetan backgrounds. Golden in color with sharp, good-looking features, a contingent of Sani women laden with goods of all types gathered in front of the hotel, lying in wait for emerging, hapless tourists. Adorned with turban-like hats containing all the colors of the rainbow, these lovely ladies are easily identified.

They had come from the Yunnan region about 50 miles away in order to take advantage of the opportunity to sell to a larger contingent of buyers. Mostly woven and embroidered clothing and large purses, the offerings were tempting. However, the women were so persistent at poking their wares in my face that I was unable to enjoy the atmosphere of casual shopping that I was looking forward to. Fully ten women surrounded me, aggressively offering their "cheap" wares. Overwhelmed, I managed to push them aside and continue walking.

The city literally stank, and a heavy pall of dirt and grime filled the air and lungs. The blocky cement buildings were unappealing and unaesthetic. I reluctantly concluded that the women were much more interesting.

Returning to the hotel, I braced myself for the phalanx of Sani at the gate. Better prepared, I asserted some order to the chaotic hawking this time and chose an embroidered, multi-colored belt. The Sanis would experience a reverse interaction several days later when we visited their home territory near the Stone Forest in Yunnan. I would share my bagpipes with them.

That evening I joined George for a walk after dinner. We set out to see the "old town" not far away. We wandered through the meandering streets of old Kunming, a startling contrast to the wide avenues of central Kunming. The row houses offered some second stories, which jutted out over their ground floors. I was reminded of the Tudor architecture found in parts of England.

I understand that the government has since destroyed much of this architecture in an effort to "modernize." I did spy an errant television, a few even in color, now and then through open doors. On dirt floors in homes with no sanitary facilities, the TVs hinted that some kind of "progress," even in 1987, had come to China in strange ways.

We continued our walk and exited from the 19th century into what was then "modern China" on the other side of old town. We turned toward the hotel but failed to find a street heading in the right direction. We continued walking in a northerly instead of an easterly direction. Nothing led back to the hotel!

After more than an hour of wandering, we were getting more and more lost. We ducked into a local hotel, inquiring as to our whereabouts. To our welcome relief, a city map was displayed on the wall. Unfortunately, we were off the map! George's limited Chinese lacked the correct dialect. So directions back to our hotel were mostly through exaggerated grunts and hand signals.

We finally made the correct easterly turn and, after several more inquiries of friendly locals who may or may not have understood us, we somehow managed to stumble upon our hotel. The planned half hour evening stroll had turned into a three-hour marathon. But experiencing Kunming at night was wonderful.

The Stone Forest, 75 miles to the northeast, is another tourist attraction, but well worth seeing, especially after the daytime tourists leave. The "forest" is, in reality, a geologic oddity of limestone formations left by a receding sea while the land uplifted. Wandering in and out, up and down the strange shapes led by a Sani guide was intriguing. Still, I found the people to be more fascinating.

The same entrepreneurial tenacity seen at the hotel in Kunming met us upon our arrival at the Stone Forest. I was convinced some of the same women from the hotel entrance had followed us, burdened with the same decorated aprons and embroidered weavings. We escaped the barrage and headed for our hotel rooms. After an almost warm shower, I elected to head down a path behind the hotel and practice my lately neglected pipes. The hustling of the bazaar was out of sight and hearing. Finally I would have some undisturbed, unobserved practice. I was surrounded by untilled land left fallow; not a soul was in sight.

After a few tunes, I detected a faint form in the distance approaching from down the path. I continued playing until I finally made out the shape of a water buffalo and its master, an old, timeless, slightly bent Chinese man with the classic inscrutable visage. Undaunted, the two of them were not to be denied use of the path, which they, no doubt, had used every day for forty years. Their pace imperceptibly slowed the closer they approached what had to be to them a strange apparition making stranger noises.

To this day, I don't know who was more unsure of whom: the water buffalo of me or me of the water buffalo. We both sidestepped the path a bit to let the other pass. Eyes glued on each other, we kept to our appointed tasks. Our heads swiveled to check for any last minute unpredictable moves as I played on.

The Chinese attendant neither smiled nor frowned, nor showed any emotion. The beast and owner seemed a good match. I was just happy that the animal had remained disinterested. It occurred to me he might think the pipes represented some kind of mating call. The two cultures had met and respected each other, though any understanding of the other was questionable. I would entertain others leading their water buffalos to unclear destinations and experience the same wariness.

Water buffalo are mostly used for tilling the rice fields. While they have been domesticated in China, the Cape buffalo of Africa, quite a different wild animal, has not.

While neither is considered aggressive, the Cape buffalo has a reputation for unpredictability and can be quite dangerous. I was not aware of any descriptions of rampaging water buffalo. Still, how many had heard bagpipes before?

By this time, three Sani women had appeared from the same direction as the man and water buffalo. George had sensed a potentially interesting encounter and joined me. He was able to provide some interpreting skills. These women were, no doubt, preparing to assist their fellow merchants down the path but decided that a few minutes with Scottish bagpipes were not to be missed.

For the first time, selling was not the only thing on their minds. They walked right up to me and plunked their faces three inches from mine. Invading someone's personal space is a common Chinese practice. When I finished with the tune, they all questioned me at once. George's expertise was stretched, but we all managed some form of informational exchange.

One wizened old woman was so taken with the sound that she invited me into her house to play. I sensed that this was a great honor. I was only too eager to follow, but pre-arranged dinner plans interfered, and I promised to make an effort to return after dinner.

Two-and-a-half hours later, I was astonished to see she was still stubbornly sitting outside the hotel entrance. She would not be denied. Upon my emergence, she leapt to her feet and clapped her hands like a six year old getting a new toy for Christmas.

I was ushered forthwith down the road to her nearby village, maybe a quarter of a mile away. The houses, more accurately described as huts, were scrunched together in the mud and offered little shelter from the elements. Yet, this persistent woman was obviously proud to have me enter.

Windowless and lightless except what the open door allowed, the hut radiated darkness, and it took some time for my eyes to adjust. I eventually spied a bed in one corner and some stored food in another. There was nothing else in the low-ceilinged hut. In the backwater homes of China, at least, apparently any furniture beyond a bed was considered superfluous, or just couldn't be afforded.

I had arranged with George to barter with this woman for some embroidery in exchange for a few tunes. He got her to agree, and I was pleased with myself that I was participating in trading the way commerce used to be conducted for so many centuries.

As soon as the deal was made, I stood up from the bed as best I could. I was glad that my 5'3" height allowed me to play without bending my knees. The drones just

brushed the ceiling when I stood. Within the first few
bars of music, the doorway was darkened with a good
portion of the rest of the village. Smiling faces thrust

Bagpipes meet a water buffalo. (photo by Dewey Webster)

themselves toward the strange music.

Without windows, the dirt walls and floor magnified
the reverberating sound, creating an ear-splitting
noise. We quickly agreed I should play out in her small
courtyard since the music was more than deafening
inside. This idea was met with great enthusiasm from
the audience. Unfortunately, I found I could hardly play
out in the open. I was crushed with curious women
pinching the bag and feeling the drones. Moving my
arms became almost impossible, as was squeezing the

bag. But I played on, loving the challenge and the unadulterated appreciation.

I began to understand that the slight, wrinkled woman initiating the entire scene was regarded as something of a village elder. She was deferred to in subtle ways and, no doubt, gained more respect for her coup of capturing a bagpiper for her own. Interestingly, out of thirty or so villagers pressing against me, I observed only two men. Questions as to the whereabouts of the other men were answered obliquely, and we never did find out where they were.

I was wearing out and time came to receive my bartered embroidered cloth. Never underestimate the clever Chinese merchant. A less impressive embroidered apron was exchanged for what I thought I was to receive. All of a sudden, these entrepreneurs found it more difficult to understand George's Chinese. I had to be happy with the idea of bartering more than the actual bartered good I received. The Sani obviously were better at this game than I would ever be. I departed with good feelings, however, and prize the remarkable experience.

The next day brought an incredible treat. As we rode our bikes back to Kunming, we happened upon an open-air Chinese market in action. The road on either side into the town was jammed solid with every type of conveyance possible and people of all kinds, especially Sani and Bai.

The Bai usually wear white clothes but with jackets of red, blue and black, embroidered belts, and loose trousers. Some women who were unmarried wore pigtails on the top of their heads; married women rolled their hair. Later, I would see their famous tie-dyes when we visited Dali.

Women of Stone Forest enjoyed the bagpipe sounds inside their home. (photo by Dewey Webster)

The constant din of voices, horns and animal squawks was actually hurtful to my ears, even to those used to hearing bagpipes! Trucks were faced nose to nose; humans were squeezed into narrow spaces between the vehicles. We were forced to dismount and walk the bikes. The others in our bus continued at a creep through the cacophony of sounds only too eager to get to the other side. At this point, I wondered why they had even come on this adventurous bike trip. George and I laid our bikes down in some grass and scrambled up an embankment to the central plaza of the town, the objective of the moving jumble of humanity in the road below.

Wares of all sorts were spread out over every inch of the football-field-sized town square. And people of all kinds were busy hustling these goods. Poles for fencing, baskets of varying shapes and sizes—some the size of the women carrying them, food of every imaginable kind—fruits and vegetables I had never seen before, cloth in a multitude of colors, and a plethora of unidentifiable things. Trading was conducted excitedly with hands moving as fast as mouths.

Ethnic dress completed the scene with women sporting bright indigo skirts and blouses, embroidered with multi-colored accents. Most weren't very keen on being photographed, but they certainly didn't hesitate to take their minds off of trading long enough to eye the only Caucasians in their midst. Bike shorts emphasized how out of place we were. We felt a bit like Martian aliens.

This was free enterprise at its best, and the Chinese were thoroughly enjoying it. The amount of free enterprise that had been suppressed by Mao Zedong was formidable. Yet this activity was obviously the life-blood of these people, and the patient Chinese had resumed the ancient tradition without missing a step.

The market provided their social time in a lifestyle that allowed very little. In spite of the spirited haggling, smiles were everywhere. My bagpipes were locked up in the bus, so this time I was the one who got to stare. George had to pull me away or I would have been the last to leave the market.

We still had 13 miles to go to reach Kunming. Dusk was approaching. The others in my group preferred the safety of staying in the bus. Again, it was the same intrepid three who committed to testing our survival skills with the Chinese and biked with the best of them. The closer we came to the city, the dirtier and grittier it got. Traffic increased, clanky noise increased, and we were in the midst of rush hour. There was as much traffic entering the city as leaving. Where everyone was going was a wonderment.

The roads widened to allow bus, truck, tractor, and bike traffic to vie for any spare inch of road—at the same time. There were some cars, but, in the late 1980s, there weren't many. At one point, I realized three vehicles were passing me at the same time! I had been weaving in and out of other bikes when I noticed a three-wheeled tractor and two trucks passing each other and me at the same moment. Fortunately, there wasn't any traffic in the opposite lane.

In spite of the growing darkness, I kept my sunglasses on. The grit in the air was so heavy and distracting, wearing contact lenses was a challenge. At least the sunglasses offered some protection. We joined more and more bikes as we reached the city center. Now city buses presented new obstacles.

I was passing one such bus that was at a bus stop only to realize that the driver had decided at that exact moment to pull out as I was alongside it. I had to use my hand on the bus to push off or I would have been knocked sideways into three other cyclists. Whether anyone would have stopped to take notice of four downed bikers was doubtful. I sped up, outdistanced the smoking vehicle, and felt grateful for my survival instincts.

Gluttons for more, George and I rode over to Green Lake after dinner. Green Lake Park itself was a particularly attractive place, with appealing landscaped trees and other colorful vegetation. We thought it a good place to sit and relax after the hair-raising rides of the day. As we walked around the lake, we heard faint sounds of music wafting over the water. Multi-colored lights reflected giddily on the ripples. We concluded that a dance was in progress and investigated.

As we approached, we saw a pavilion crowded with young girls and boys dancing to a live band playing mildly raucous, Western-style dance music that wasn't really quite yet rock. The procedure seemed to involve buying to buy tickets at a booth across the way and presenting them at the pavilion door.

We were eager to experience a Chinese dance and proceeded to step up to the booth. Again, George experienced some language difficulties. After some hesitation and hand waving, we purchased our tickets. However, upon presentation at the dance entrance, our tickets were refused. We were denied entrance into the dance. In faintly understood Chinese, we were told that this dance was for Chinese; we should go to the dance at our hotel, the Kunming Hotel.

George was stunned. It was the first time in several trips to China he had ever encountered xenophobia. Eventually, we were offered our money back. We decided instead to give our tickets to the surprised Chinese couple next in line.

We scratched our heads in disbelief and ended up at the hotel dance. This one was for tourists and had quite a different flavor. The Chinese here were dressed fashionably and strained to watch our every move. If they wanted to see the latest Western dance styles, we were not good role models. We barely remembered our '60s moves while the Chinese were up to the '70s, if not beyond.

8
SURVIVING THE DRIVE TO DALI AND LIJIANG

Xiaguan, on the way to Lijiang, was a long, scary eight-hour roller coaster drive with Mr. Suh, our kamikaze bus driver, at the wheel. The trip would have taken perhaps 10-12 hours for any sane driver.

The group's farthest west destination was Lijiang, a town north and west of Kunming. The 11-hour road trip covering more than 500 miles was daunting but well worth the effort. I found the bus ride to be more than heart palpitating. We zoomed through small towns without an inkling of slowing down and viewed periodic bus wrecks down the embankments of our road. The drivers in China do not have "safety first" on their minds. Their objective seems to be simply to arrive at the destination as quickly as possible, with little regard for other traffic or existing road conditions.

As long as the driver leaned on the horn, it was full speed ahead. As I mentioned previously, honking horns apparently exonerate drivers of any responsibility toward pedestrians. And passing anything slower was an automatic immediate reaction, regardless of any oncoming traffic or turns in the road. The game of "chicken" was in their genes. I forced my view sideways to divert my attention to the ubiquitous terraced rice fields. Mozart's "Requiem" on the tape player also helped.

Xiaguan, on the way to Lijiang, was a long, scary eight-hour roller coaster drive with Mr. Suh, our kamikaze bus driver, at the wheel. The trip would have taken perhaps 10-12 hours for any sane driver. Improved roads since 1987 have eased the drive to perhaps five hours today. Here was another bustling burg of many thousands, many more than I had expected for a town so remote.

Dali is really considered the old town of Xiaguan, with a population of 40,000. But the entire Dali prefecture now has more than three million plus people. We reached farther and farther into the "outback," and still we experienced large cities complete with stores selling the latest Western goods.

While taking the obligatory reconnaissance walk around town that night, we discovered a local talent show. In a large city auditorium, amateur hour was in full swing. A strange talent show it was! The capacity audience rarely clapped. Perhaps that was because the acts were so terrible: semi-go-go dancers reminding me of the 1960s but not quite in sync; jugglers missing whatever it was they were juggling; and acrobats fresh out of elementary school, not quite able to make the double back flip. The go-go dancers were particularly interesting because China in 1987 was still just coming out of its thaw of the 1970s regarding relations with the West. But even the magic tricks failed to excite the crowd.

Several in the audience were quite keen to offer their seats to us. They seemed to be complimented and thrilled that we would be interested in their show. However, we found it difficult to maintain any enthusiasm for the less than professional renditions of song and dance and left as unobtrusively as possible.

Group travel is a psychological study in itself. Passengers in travel groups are unknown to each other before the trip and are thrown together from various locations and complicated backgrounds. After even just one week, a group either consolidates or disintegrates. The honeymoon among the passengers is over and the true personalities emerge, especially under the stress of all the hassles travel has to offer.

At first, group members usually make great efforts to overlook the idiosyncrasies of each other. As time and the pressures of travel progress, whatever social skills people possess weaken. It's difficult to put up with a fellow passenger's constant jabbering or another's never-ending complaints while you're struggling with an upset stomach.

By the end of the second week, groups usually have factionalized, sometimes into two major camps, sometimes into several smaller cliques. Unique personalities and the size of the group, as well as the skills of the group leader, help to determine the direction this goes. These tensions can be a distraction to enjoying the new cultures and may require judiciously placed blinders to maintain equanimity.

In our case, we mostly broke off into pairs. George and I provided solace for each other while the two younger gals kept to themselves. Bill, the architect, teamed up with our cute Chinese interpreter. The husband of the newly married couple had become so obnoxious I tried to pretend he was not a part of us. The rest of our group fell between the cracks.

The faulty plumbing at our hotel, which should have been only a minor irritation, only intensified ill feelings. Hot water was unknown here in Xiaguan. In fact, we were lucky to get running water at all from our showers. I was on my way out the hotel doors, bagpipes in hand, when I heard our medical intern berate the confused Chinese concierge for not having the correct change for his laundry bill. I had to wonder: Why do some people travel to faraway places and still expect American standards everywhere? It is a question often asked about American travelers.

I escaped to a lonely spot by the bank of the nearby river in the growing dusk of the evening. I had become frustrated with the group and prized some time alone. Bagpiping can be as effective at purging the body of ills and psychological stresses as jogging or physical exercise.

I played all the tunes I knew and was only vaguely aware of the crowd that had lined the nearby bridge, which overlooked my space. I was gratified that they applauded with more enthusiasm than I'd heard at the talent show!

Some nerves were calmed during our boat ride on Erhai Lake the next morning. A skitterish sun accompanied us the length of the lake for the three-hour trip. A stop at a Buddhist shrine on an island convinced us that expression of religion was beginning to be tolerated in an otherwise communist-dictated atheistic state. Here, three yuan, or less than a dollar, bought a stick that we pulled from a collection held by the Buddhist monk. The number on the stick corresponded to a number on a paper that told us our fortune. Our interpreter had a very strenuous time translating everyone's paper. I've often wondered if anyone gets a bad fortune in those situations.

When we disembarked, the Bai people immediately swarmed over us in the same merciless way the Sanis had when selling goods. I again reminded myself that this trade was an ancient custom, and I should not be repulsed simply because I was unused to goods being literally pushed in my face. At one point, a nondescript metal bracelet was thrust upon me with protestations of "no pay." I reluctantly accepted, suspecting duplicity, only to have the seller dog my steps for the next half hour with her hand out for any money. She refused to take back the bracelet, and I finally relented by finding some coins for her. They do have the technique perfected.

The town at the end of the lake was a distinctly small village with dirt streets, no cars, and was very quiet. I was glad to have finally found something that could be described as "quaint."

Lunch was one of the best of the trip in a quite disreputable-looking hovel. I never saw anything throughout China that resembled the chow mein and chop suey that we have here in the United States. Lunch that day was no exception. The fresh vegetables and recognizable chicken dish spiced as only the Chinese can do were a welcome relief from what seemed like the snake and dog meat we may have been eating up to now.

We had arranged to have our bikes driven in a van to the end of the lake. So, we were able to ride back to Xiaguan at our own speed, which meant I was one of the last to drag in, not because I was so slow, but because I stopped so much to enjoy the sights. Again, some Buddhist structures along the way spoke of a slightly increasing tolerance of religion.

The group was becoming growing irksome, and I set out on my own the next day. To my surprise, George suggested I bike to Dali by myself while the group spent the morning at a nearby garden park. He didn't have to twist my arm. At 9:00 a.m., I was off across the bridge where the crowd had stood enjoying the bagpipe music the night before.

Heading up the road eight miles, I stopped in the well-known town of Dali. Founded before Christ, Dali is a walled city that has attracted many tourists. It once was the capital of a powerful kingdom that ruled Yunnan for five centuries. Still, it had retained its own identity and character through the centuries. Its history is clouded with one takeover after another, and elements of Islam are still found in writing over restaurants and in the faces of the populace.

I again reminded myself that this trade was an ancient custom...

I have to admit to having some trepidation on my bike ride. My disappearance would have been untraceable in all likelihood. Finding the route was no trouble. Still, once again, I was the only Caucasian in the crowd of bikes going into Xiaguan for work. When I stopped at a small outdoor food market on the way, I found the strange animal parts that were being sold a little disconcerting. Attempts to take furtive photos of the sale of pigs' heads sloppily dressed out on benches were misguided. The Chinese were not happy with being photographed and let me know it.

However, children could usually be depended on to ham it up for cameras—something I have found to be pretty universal worldwide. I was stared at so blatantly by the adults, I couldn't "sneak" anything in the way of photos of them. Yet I never felt in danger. Perhaps I was too enthralled by the scenes I encountered to be fully aware of my precarious situation. However, I believe that I really was not in danger of any kind. Even the traffic here was bearable and posed no threat.

Upon entering Dali, I realized I was immediately in a different situation. I suddenly saw other white faces. From where they came, I don't know, perhaps on buses from Xiaguan or the few lodgings available in Dali. Some of the euphoria of the morning was dampened. Dali was on the tourist track; its charm was mitigated by efforts to please the foreigner.

After locking up the bike and making a quick tour of the stores, I bought some tie-dye material to have made into a skirt at home where everyone isn't a size four as in China. I enjoy finding places in other countries that haven't been "found" yet by tourists. Those places are becoming harder to discover. Yet I'm hopeful that the increased travel by people from all around the world is helping those people understand other cultures even as some parts of those cultures may be disappearing.

I ducked into an inauspicious-looking compound advertising baths and massages in English. I had heard about this opportunity from a previous guest and had sought out the 60-cent massage. In spite of a few minor issues, I was not to regret my decision. Notwithstanding the English sign out front, no one seemed to understand a word of anything I said. But they did take my money and prepared me for a massage. I was taken to a semi-sordid room—the rooms were separated by gender—where a female motioned me to undress while a huge, freestanding bathtub of questionable cleanliness was filled.

Slipping into the hot natural mineral water and generally kicking back to work out the tension of dealing with the group was my focus. The soaking was enjoyable but overly prolonged. After fifty minutes, I tired of waiting for a sign for my next step. Besides, I was shriveled, having taken on a prunish appearance and was thoroughly warmed. I gingerly stepped out of the old cast-iron tub, dried myself and waited, and waited. Another 15 minutes passed, and I inched toward the doorway with a towel judiciously placed and motioned to a figure far away in another building.

The female attendant finally arrived and cursorily plopped me down on another cot of questionable cleanliness and proceeded to give me a dedicated and strenuous massage. I have taken a few massage classes, enjoyed several massages up to that point, and have read some books on the matter. So I was curious to note her technique as well as benefit from it. She worked largely from her fingertips and seemed quite competent.

Shortly, I became less of a student and more of a customer. Having been lulled into another state of being, I was startled back into reality when she abruptly popped my finger joints one at a time. The other hand was done in quick succession. By the time she got to my toes, I was starting to brace for what was less than a totally pleasant sensation.

As I was recovering from the joint cracking, I felt a very hot balm being rubbed all over my back. Was this the real "tiger balm" spoken of so highly in all the literature and travel books? She placed a warm towel over the balm, which increased the heat sensation four-fold. The feeling verged on being unpleasant, but had the effect of wakening my body.

I emerged from my experience feeling very tingly and a bit debilitated. I had been concerned about the risk of entering into another world, but for 60 cents the experience was worth it. I reluctantly met the group for lunch and braced myself for the increasing tension with the larger group.

Another three to four hours saw us in Lijiang. The reckless driving habits of our bus driver only amplified the tensions within the group, but the countryside of endlessly rolling rice terraces had a soothing effect. Lijiang is where the Jade River divides into three rivers. It contains an old town whose antiquity was easily relished.

In the early to mid-1600s, a "Chinese Indiana Jones" by the name of XuXiake devoted his life to his sense of wanderlust and love of the strange, taking on the poetic nom de plume, "Traveler in the Sunset Clouds." He reached the area of Yunnan, which is now more and more popular with tourists, but was very difficult to reach in 1636. He had planned a four-year journey to explore the mountains, valleys, and Buddhist monasteries and to experience the diversity of cultures along the way. He described Lijiang beneath the Jade Dragon Snow Mountain and the Naxi people as idyllic.

Unfortunately, according to the very informative article, "Traveler in the Sunset Clouds," in *Smithsonian* magazine in its April 2015 edition, Lijiang has "reinvented" itself as a "raucous party town" and demonstrated everything that "can go wrong with Chinese tourism." The author, Tony Perrottet, was able to get a taste of the old Lijiang when he visited Xuan Ke, who was imprisoned for 21 years during the Communist era. He is a classical musician on the *guqin,* a zither-like stringed instrument. In spite of the changes, classical music has apparently managed to survive in Yunnan. Unfortunately,

I never got to discover how these musicians would have taken to bagpipes.

Perrottet further depresses the reader by describing how a highway has marred the Tiger Leaping Gorge, clogging the viewpoints with tourist buses. Similarly, Dali has transformed into a "Chinese hippie hangout." He even likens the place to my present hometown of Boulder, Colorado! While identifying with XuXiake's spirit of curiosity, I am grateful I could enjoy Lijiang and Dali before the hordes of tourists changed these enjoyable towns.

Riddled with cobblestoned streets, Lijiang is difficult to navigate with a bike. Walking is advised. Here we found the Naxi people with distinctive dress, which included long gowns and colorful, embroidered sheepskin capes. Again, blue is the preferred color for dress. Closing in on the Tibetan border, we heard a rumor that the bus ride to Lhasa was "only" a two-week ride!

After our late afternoon arrival, I was hoping to find places suitable for biking. The size of Lijiang was more manageable than the huge cities we had encountered so far. It contained one million people in 2010, considerably fewer in 1987. I managed to ride from the hotel to the old town, through a winding maze of those narrow, widely spaced cobblestoned streets waiting to eat bikes. In a short time, I admitted defeat, dismounted, and walked my bike.

The scenes encountered could have been from a century ago. With large windows open to the narrow lanes, I was able to see dentists performing extractions and other such procedures with primitive tools. Beauty parlors offered permanents with their convoluted machinery practically in the street. And, finally, after negotiating the knobby streets, I came upon the small village square in the midst of the old section.

I was tempted to buy a wonderfully authentic fur vest from one of the local Tibetan-looking merchants, but the smell was a bit overpowering, and I was concerned that it wouldn't be well-received by my companions. I was unsuccessful trying to find out which animal had provided the fur. Our group's best guess was that it was some kind of bear.

Perhaps if I had had the foresight to carry my bagpipes with me, I could have managed a better bargain. I did buy some brass goblets and doorknockers; unfortunately, I have never found a use for any of the items. I finally threw them away after moving them from one home to another too many times. But the seller's diminutive pet monkey, which scrambled all over his kiosk trading kisses with its owner, captured my heart and I was a pushover for a sale. Never mind that the goods turned out to be useless.

In the evening, while our group played poker, I took advantage of a truly magical evening. I made one right turn out of the hotel and headed straight toward the Jade Dragon Snow Mountains, 10,000 feet above us. With a name like that, how could one not be drawn to them? The clouds had obscured the major portion of these peaks all day. Glimpses were the best I could get.

Chinese were better at bargaining than I would ever be.
(photo by Dewey Webster)

A soaking rain settled in the next day, and we left a day early to return to Kunming. I was the only person to encourage staying. I really liked the serene atmosphere and hoped we might get an unobstructed view of the mountains if the weather cleared.

Meanwhile, for this evening, I soaked up the afterglow in the fields below the little-explored mountains. Bagpipes were furthest from my mind. I felt a strange peace from a country so wrought with unstated grumblings. There was some stability in the endless lifestyle unaltered for so many centuries. Had I known that this way of life would change so quickly in the 1990s and afterwards, I might have appreciated it even more.

The China portion of our trip was winding down now. The bus retraced our steps to Xiaguan, passing another market. This time, in my haste to see everything, as I leapt off the bus, I was sideswiped by a dead pig's nose lying across a cart being pulled by that old bent man I'd seen in so many places in China. The shriveled, cane-like form of a man obliviously pushed the cart through the crowded masses.

I took one last bike ride in Kunming in the rain, lengthening the time away from the group. But the dinner was our last in China and a ceremony was planned, courtesy of the Yunnan Sports Service. Two head administrators, along with Mr. Li, our liaison, who had picked up a girlfriend somewhere between Lijiang and Kunming, were in attendance. The girlfriend had just shown up in the front seat one morning with no introduction or explanation.

Mr. Suh, our kamikaze bus driver, Xiao Fan, our ever-faithful interpreter, and the entire group were treated to a special dinner. We were presented with the prize of the evening, which was, of course t-shirts with our own special logo: "Yunnan Sparts Service." So much for Chinese editing!

I was not to play my pipes again in China. I did play when we arrived in Hong Kong, but Hong Kong was not officially a part of China in 1987, being subject to British rule instead. Were I to return, I would endeavor to play even more than I did. Playing the pipes was a wonderful way to interact with the Chinese people, and I have many fond memories as a direct result of having done so.

9

WINDING DOWN
IN HONG KONG

*Playing bagpipes nude on a beach near Hong Kong
just seemed like the thing to do at the time.*

e left the next day for Hong Kong, which is
another world from China. In 1997, when
Hong Kong was returned to China after
the British control of more than 150 years,
promises were made to maintain Hong Kong as it was
under British rule, i.e. freedom of speech and capitalism
would rule the day. Those who assumed this would hold
true under the Communist rule were to be disappointed.

A few years passed in relative tranquility, until the Communists slowly started to make political changes. Riots in 2012 and 2013 rocked the area with the future very uncertain. The disparities between Hong Kong and mainland China were particularly astonishing and positively staggering in 1987.

We came from a country mired at that time in the 19th century to a country enjoying all the fruits of the 20th century. From hovels to high rises, China was to absorb Hong Kong as a shiny brightness to their otherwise dreary drabness. China has come a long way in catching up to the modern world, but Hong Kong and mainland China may never be able to blend.

Never very comfortable at four or five star hotels, I did my best to adjust to the unaccustomed luxuries of just such a place. The travel company wanted to make our last impression of them a favorable one. The computerized television with video games and mini bar in the room were relatively new amenities at that time. But I exited our room quickly to purchase a hand-made silk dress down the street from a reputable tailor. After choosing the material and style, I would return in four hours to pick up the completed dress!

Unbelievably but predictably, the next day the group opted for a bus tour of the city. Another bus! After so many hours in a bus in the recent days? The other options were far more appealing to me. Avoiding buses was foremost in my planning. George knew of a remote beach "across the way." Without so much as a farewell to the others, George and I headed for the Toad and Frog Pub near his remote beach.

George vaguely remembered the circuitous route. A ferry ride to Kowloon, then another hour-long ride brought us to Cheun Chau Island. His memory faded at this point. As we walked along the dock, we incredulously spied a sampan owner's t-shirt with the words "Toad and Frog" on it! The sampan (flat bottomed Chinese wooden boat) owner was only too happy to take us to a classic South Seas island beach, as removed from the clogged streets of Hong Kong as any beach in Fiji could be.

We had all day to relax on the basically deserted beach with ships passing in the distance as a vague reminder of where we were. After a short swim in the warm pleasant water, we realized swimming suits were not required. This was, indeed, an empty beach of several hundred yards with not a soul in sight.

Playing bagpipes nude on a beach near Hong Kong just seemed like the thing to do at the time. Hong Kong plays host to perhaps ten local bagpipe bands, which is not surprising given its British history. Who knows? I may not have been the only one to try this. The pipes were playing well, and I found it not at all difficult to revel in the scene.

Wading in the water, I played all the tunes I knew and a few I didn't know so well. I felt a different sense of power and freedom. Playing in the nude was certainly a lot easier than playing wrapped up in nine yards of woolen kilt! To date, that is the only place I have played bagpipes *au naturel*, and I can't imagine choosing a better spot to do so.

Realizing that the day was advancing and that, indeed, some other people might appear at any given moment, I dressed and George led the way into shore a few hundred yards through some camouflaging vegetation to find what could only be termed a local pub known to a select few. No signs indicated this unique place existed. You had to know it was there to find it, and, fortunately, George had been there before.

We were quickly transported into what seemed like a place out of time. It emanated a Caribbean flavor, and I expected to see Hemingway relaxing in a corner slumped over his drink. This was our last day, and after a few gin and tonics, a hamburger and French fries, I felt sadly removed from the past four weeks in China.

With some regrets at not having more time to travel in China, I was ready to look forward to my next leg—four weeks in Japan. After another short swim with suits, we met our sampan. We had arranged for it to pick us up and we returned the way we'd come. But our psyches were revived and renewed. Our group broke up the next morning, each going his or her own way.

10

HIKING THROUGH THE JAPANESE ALPS

… the Japanese hot bath has no rivals. Here in the United States, we are beset with jets, bubbles, waterfalls, and other distractions to occupy our attention. In Japan it's a spiritual experience, and the motions of washing beforehand while drinking tea or sake as a precursor or accompaniment are analogous to the washing of the mind.

In keeping with my desire to enjoy some travel without the hassle of the day-to-day logistical planning, and in order to enjoy the company of others, I had arranged through another outdoor adventure outfit to meet a new group for a three week hiking trip through the Japanese Alps. I had six days between my last day in Hong Kong and the first day of the trip in Japan. I had no idea what I would do with those days; being alone in Tokyo was a bit intimidating.

I refrained from worrying about the particulars until I arrived in Hong Kong. I had pre-booked a flight to Tokyo, and that was as far as my planning had taken me. I now faced meeting another group with much trepidation, given my experience with the China group, but rationally I knew that personalities within a group are the luck of the draw.

By happy coincidence, our leader George was booked on the same flight to Tokyo. He was guiding another group on a bike trip in western Japan. He also had some free days. So it seemed natural to us that we should spend those days together. Besides, I mentioned my determination to climb Mt. Fuji, Fujiyama, or Fujisan—all names referring to the same perfectly conical 12,388-foot volcanic peak outside of Tokyo. The idea had appealed to him, too. Not only did he speak fluent Japanese, he had spent several years in Japan teaching English to Japanese. So here I was, with a private, experienced guide, and great company as well, while solving the question as to what to do with the next six days.

I quickly learned how lucky I was to have such company as soon as I retrieved my luggage. The airport is not adjacent to the city; the trip at that time required about two hours. As it turned out, George's route was a stroke of sheer genius and would have been impossible for me to figure out by myself. Our route, which involved transferring from a bus to a train to a subway to a taxi in one-and-a-half hours for a reasonable sum, was impressive.

Of course, years later on a subsequent trip to Japan, I took a speedy train directly into Tokyo. Yes, it was efficient but certainly not as adventurous. I'm sure I could have found some hotel bus to take me into the city charging three times what we eventually spent. But our journey into the city was much more interesting than a simple bus ride. It also was an early education into the transportation magic of Japan. I learned quickly not to fear the subway system, but it helped to have someone along who was familiar with the scene. The subway is incredibly efficient; you just have to have the confidence to know how to use it.

As it is, in many cities, the subway system is color coded and not difficult to navigate. However, I found that when I traveled there in 2005, I was turning into a troglodyte from using the subway so much. The dark, cavernous sameness led one to forget there was an outside. Fortunately, we were now to move outside of the city on our quest to climb Mt. Fuji and enjoy the sunlight.

When we arrived in downtown Tokyo, we opted for a *ryokan,* or inn, in the Akasaka section of Tokyo recommended off-handedly by a fellow tourist in the airport. The inauspicious lodging was in keeping with the Japanese lifestyle and philosophy. From the outside, the inn was barely distinguishable from a family home. However, the inside immediately removed the guest from the outside world.

A sense of peace enveloped me as I stepped through the door. Exactly what induces this feeling is intangible, but it's there. I was shown to my room up three flights of stairs. My first night in Japan was spent on a tatami mat with warm lightweight quilts. The anteroom had a low table set for tea and the traditional cotton Japanese robe or *yukata* folded neatly in anticipation of a bath.

I had no choice but to stop and leisurely enjoy the tea and bath. It's what keeps one sane in the frenetic pace of outside. Contrary to many *ryokans,* this one had a private bath. And I experienced one of the finest customs in the world. After soaping up from a small bucket of water from a bamboo pail and washing well with a small terry cloth towel, I rinsed several times before sinking into the hot water of the deep Japanese tub to soak for as long as I wished. I would use the same minimal terry cloth towel, wrung out, to dry myself.

Similar to, but in ways very different from, our hot tubs, Jacuzzis, and whirlpools, the Japanese hot bath has no rivals. Here in the United States, we are beset with jets, bubbles, waterfalls, and other distractions to occupy our attention. In Japan it's a spiritual experience, and the motions of washing beforehand while drinking tea or sake as a precursor or accompaniment are analogous to the washing of the mind.

Not to demean the hot springs or hot tubs in the U.S., I have enjoyed some of the best, from natural hot springs in Steamboat Springs, Colorado, to the Salt Flats Natural Springs in eastern Oregon, to hot tubs in posh resorts, but there is an incomparable peace to the Japanese baths. Needless to say, that night I fell into a deep and restful sleep.

Surprisingly, even in light of George's expertise in the Japanese language, we found it difficult to decipher the maze of routes to the town of Kawaguchi-ko at the base of Mt. Fuji. After several inquiries that were met with incomplete replies, we managed to connect two subway rides and two train rides to our destination.

While on one of the train rides, I noticed a curious situation. George and I were sitting on one side of a compartment when a Japanese family consisting of mother, father, son, and daughter came on board. Seats were scarce, and they approached our area. There were only two seats for the four of them. Without a moment's hesitation, the father and son sat down while the mother and daughter were left standing. There was no question as to who was given preference.

However, I have heard that, behind the scenes at home, the wife usually handles the money and is the force behind the show. Things may have changed since then, but appearances aren't always what they seem.

Mt. Fuji has ten "stations" on its slopes, each with one or more huts at each station. The fifth station is at 8,000 ft. and is the end of the winding road for the buses. We spent the night at the base in Kawaguchi-ko at a *minshuku*, a B-rated *ryokan*, and waited for the first bus in the morning to the fifth station.

By 11:20 a.m. we were at the fifth station and on the more than well-beaten trail to Mt. Fuji's summit. Hailed as a spiritual pilgrimage in Japan, this majestic volcanic peak holds a mystique for locals and foreigners alike.

Perfectly conical in shape, it rises ethereally more than 12,000 feet from the surrounding area. Often hidden in clouds, the summit feels the affects of the nearby Pacific Ocean.

Once known as a sister peak to Mt. St. Helens in Washington before St. Helens erupted in 1980 and blew 2,000 feet off its top, Mt. Fuji may be the most climbed mountain in the world. Mt. Monadnock in New Hampshire lays claim to being the most climbed, with 120,000 hikers per year. However, that claim doesn't approach the 253,414 that climbed Mt. Fuji in one year's premier two-month climbing season on the main trail.

The middle of September saw fewer numbers clambering up its slopes than usual. In fact, the huts apparently shut down around our Labor Day and activity becomes bearable for those wanting to enjoy a little more peace and quiet. The experience of climbing Mt. Fuji was not so magical. It is, in fact, a huge cinder cone. If hiking off trail, you frequently take one step up and slide down two, rolling on the small volcanic cinders.

So many thousands have made the effort, though, that steps have worked their way into the side of the mountain, and upward movement can be maintained. Late fall, winter, and early spring ascents on snow would present a much different proposition, however. Now, we had only to concentrate on putting one foot in front of the other.

We were blessed with good weather and reached the summit in less than five hours. Abandoned sellers' booths lined up at the crest of the summit were a stark reminder that a climb of Mt. Fuji is not a wilderness experience. I rejoiced that I was there after the tourist season and did not have to walk by the barrage of souvenir shops.

The summit crater is fairly extensive, and we had time to circumnavigate it. The spiritual summit to the east of the now invisible vendors' booths was adorned with tori gates and we respectfully approached. The wind was mild but noticeable. Dusk was approaching and I realized my opportunity was quickly fading.

I had dreamed of playing my bagpipes on the top of Mt. Fuji since I had started learning the pipes. I was trembling as I removed them from my daypack and put the drones together. I hoped that I wasn't intruding upon the deities, but rather showing them respect.

Playing pipes at 12,388 feet is a struggle at best. The oxygen I needed to blow up the bag would be significantly less at this altitude and only the first problem. The cold wind numbed my fingers as I squawked out the first notes. The reeds told me that they were not happy. In fact, I've never heard such caterwauling from bagpipes before! It reminded me of the tired old joke, "Why do bagpipers always walk when they play? To get away from the sound!"

I briefly took the pipes apart and examined the reeds and tried to work

I had created this magical image of playing my bagpipes on the top of Mt. Fuji.

some magic into them. All was for naught. I never could elicit a real bagpipe sound. I was devastated. I had created this magical image of playing my bagpipes on the top of Mt. Fuji. Perhaps the deities weren't as happy about the proposition as I thought they would be.

I tried to play to the deities on top of Mt. Fuji.
(photo by Dewey Webster)

Reluctantly, I packed the pipes away and we headed over to the permanent weather station on the far side of the crater. By now, we were two of only a handful of visitors at the top. In spite of the disappointment with the pipes, the experience of exploring Mt. Fuji's summit was rewarding. I had no idea a hiker could actually hike around the crater in about an hour and see a weather station on the way. The view from the top offered a different and impressive perspective of Japan, to be sure.

Knowing that the mountain means so much to the Japanese added a special flavor to being there. I felt the awe the Japanese held for the peak. Signs of man are everywhere, from the vendor booths to the weather station to tori gates to rocks laid out spelling words. Still, the growing twilight and quiet instilled a sense of humility in me.

Sunset found us retracing our steps down. We stopped at the eighth station, which had stayed open only to house a construction crew working on an addition to the hut. We were served an adequate meal and retired, happy to have experienced the climb and only a little regretful at the poor bagpipe show.

We were awakened at 5:00 a.m. for the much sought-after sunrise from Mt. Fuji. Seeing sunrise on Mt. Fuji is a must for all Japanese. Incredibly, every one of the construction crew roused themselves to see what they'd no doubt seen so many times before. We lined the deck in time to watch a brilliant sun creep over the horizon. There was a quiet magic about the scene. I was convinced the Japanese felt something from the view that I could not. Still, my appreciation of the unique experience was deep.

Everyone fell back to sleep for a few more hours before actually rising for the day's work. As we descended, we met quite a number of climbers on their way up. "Konichiwa" which means "hello" or "good afternoon" greeted us from each one; or, in most cases, it was just "wa." Going down on cinders is much easier than ascending, and we reached the fifth station for a late breakfast.

The bus into town wouldn't leave until noon, and we considered our options: mill around for a few hours or hitchhike. Ambling around the parking lot, George spied a thirtyish Japanese man with a New York Yankees baseball cap approaching his car. Politely and carefully, George struck up a conversation in Japanese only to discover that they each knew the same farm family with whom George had spent a summer homestay 25 years before! He was only too happy to drive us down and babbled all the way in mixed Japanese and English. He had lived in the U.S for a year and seemed totally comfortable with us.

11
ANOTHER GROUP!

"Smoke, there is one thing you should know about me before we start." His shoulders visibly tensed. "I play the bagpipes and would like to bring them along."

He stopped mid-stride for only the briefest instant. "If you really want to carry them with you, that's okay." The response seemed terse, but I felt an ever-so-slight smile in those words.

B ack in Tokyo, I was facing the prospect of meeting my second travel group for part two of my adventure. The last few days had been ideal and my preferred way to travel. But I was eager to do some long-term hiking, however, and my new group was ready to leave for the mountains. I said farewell to George who had been so instrumental in helping me realize my goal of climbing Mt. Fuji. We have remained friends ever since and stay in contact, keeping track of each other's travels.

The group had already been together for two days when I managed to catch up with them after my extended respite between group trips. I met my roommate first, as I stumbled into our hotel room after my Mt. Fuji success. Mary was Canadian, in her late thirties, an experienced traveler and a high-powered upper management type at her business. Almost before any amenities were attended to, she warned me about the other four ladies who comprised our small group. Oh boy! Just what I needed—more tension from egos.

Three flight attendants in their mid to late forties seemed nice but were dubious hikers. Mary said that they just didn't look like they were in very good shape. Another lady in her fifties was a different story. Dingy from head to toe, she had managed to estrange herself from everyone already. Clingy and batty, Tillie had little or no hiking experience, nor was she in any kind of physical condition to undertake a major hiking trip. I was not encouraged with the news, to say the least.

Would this be another experience I would have to enjoy in spite of the group? I was too flush with the enjoyment of the last few days to want to dwell on the bleak possibility. Besides, first impressions are notoriously flawed. I hoped this would be the case.

I showered, not totally ecstatic with the modern high-rise hotel. My mind wandered back to the joys of my nights in the *ryokan.* I had only minutes to get ready to meet our leader, who, by this time, was scratching his head over my late arrival.

It is trite to say that Smoke Blanchard was a legend in his time, but he was unabashedly proud of that description. The author of *Walking Up and Down in the World (*Sierra Club Books, 1985*),* Smoke had been a truck driver by trade. Along the way, he became one of the original professional mountain guides in this country. Establishing the Palisades School of Mountaineering out of Bishop, California, he taught climbing in one of the first climbing schools out West.

Smoke went on to lead hiking and climbing groups around the world as well as becoming a specially well-respected mountaineer. He was 72 years old when I met him, with legs like tree stumps that belied his snow-white beard and hair. His fortyish Japanese girlfriend was added testimony to his youthful attitude and joy of living.

He seemed curiously befuddled when I met him in the lobby of the hotel, minutes from his and Keiko's apartment. He fumbled with papers and disjointedly discussed the trip. My impression was less than positive, but as I said, first impressions can be misleading. I had heard just enough about the man to hold some awe in reserve, just in case.

Years before, a friend had signed on to an expedition in Africa with him to climb Mt. Kenya, a more technical climb than the better-known Mt. Kilimanjaro. My friend's assessment was that he "would go anywhere with him." In the meantime, I wondered if he might be too old to continue leading paying customers on travels. I quickly discovered that my reserved awe would come in handy.

After the cursory descriptions of what might or might not happen on our trip, he took me next door to a bookstore to buy some maps. He seemed to become more relaxed perusing the shelves. So I ventured to approach the subject on my mind. "Smoke, there is one thing you should know about me before we start." His shoulders visibly tensed. "I play the bagpipes and would like to bring them along."

He stopped mid-stride for only the briefest instant. "If you really want to carry them with you, that's okay." The response seemed terse, but I felt an ever-so-slight smile in those words. During the trip, he was to enjoy the pipes as much or more than anyone. Perhaps he was glad for the novelty after leading so many less experienced clients on one trip after another. He had made this particular hike from hut to hut in the Japanese Alps many times, and the added distraction of bagpipes seemed just fine with him.

Traveling with six women seemed just fine with him, too. In fact, he commented that women were usually the better travelers, with fewer complaints. Women had no macho image to live up to and generally had better attitudes. Our small entourage braved the morning subways with backpacks in tow. We managed to board the train together and headed to Matsumoto, a town less than four hours away to the west. From Ariake, the next destination by train, we took a 45-minute taxi ride up to a hot springs and our *minshuku*.

12

INTO THE WILD

When I finished the tune, we heard yells and noise from a group down below outside the hut. Had I gone too far and disturbed the tranquility of the Japanese Alps? A friendly Japanese man at the top set me straight and offered the information in English. He said they were yelling the equivalent of "encore" in Japanese!

O ur 17-day hike had officially begun, and I could think of no better way to commemorate the occasion than by wandering off into the forest that evening to play my pipes. The three flight attendants had closeted themselves in their own room filled with tatami mats to catch up on recent experiences since, while they were employed by the same airline carrier, they did not see much of each other.

Mary, my roommate, quickly established her preference for aloneness, and Tillie was to be avoided at all costs. Smoke needed some time to organize and made it clear he was not in the business to entertain us. He would guide us and look out for our safety; he would not mother hen us.

The natural hot springs were a welcome relief after I spent some time in the drizzly woods playing. It was almost too cold to keep my fingers moving with any kind of accuracy. I think I just wanted to initiate my pipes and myself to a Japan that wasn't 12,388 feet in elevation. The pipes were hesitant to recover from their experience on Mt. Fuji. But the lower elevation helped, and I had a good time playing in the mists of Japan. No others were around, and I could convince myself no one else could hear me. This time I could really get some good practice.

When I returned to the *ryokan*, I discovered that the three-quarters of a mile I had hiked out from our lodging had not been sufficient to contain the sounds of a bagpipe. The flight attendants found out for the first time that they had a bagpiper amongst them. Fortunately, they seemed happy for the added oddity.

They chorused that they all liked the sound. I tried
not to think about what the evening's damp weather
portended for our next day's hike. For now, I felt good
after piping in the woods and soaking in a natural bath
in the mountains of Japan.

The next 17 days would see few baths and, fortunately,
little rain when we hiked. More than primed, I waited
at the trailhead for the group. By now, I had discerned
that the flight attendants had had hiking experiences
in Nepal and around the world. They may not have
looked the part, but they turned out to be great troopers
and fun companions. Tilly, on the other hand, was a
bit scary. She was, in fact, totally out of her element. A
bridge party would have been more suitable for her.

We enthusiastically charged up a steep muddy trail.
From the maps, I could see that our first day would be
a challenge. I knew enough to pace myself from the
beginning. Smoke helped. In fact, the incredibly steady
pace he set throughout our daily hikes was a constant
marvel. I felt like I could have continued at that speed
for days without stopping.

I used to have a hiking partner who consistently
stayed a mile ahead of me. He would eventually stop
and rest, waiting for me to catch up. When I finally
arrived, panting and exhausted, and even before I sat

down, up he'd jump and take off, expecting me to follow immediately. Now I found out just how enjoyable hiking could be without gasping for air every step of the way endeavoring to keep up with a speedy hiking partner.

Tillie obviously was not of the same mind. Not more than one-half mile up the trail, she started to complain. She was toward the back of the group from the start. She turned to me saying simply, "I don't think I can make it. Does it get any easier?" Not wanting to encourage her, I could honestly say that today was likely to be tough all the way to the first hut.

Another client on the hike had made the same trip a few years before. She confirmed what I said only in stronger terms, and for the same reason. She had spent her last trip to Japan suffering the company of a similar malcontent hiker and couldn't conceive of having to do it again. In truth, neither one of us wanted Tillie's unpleasant company on the trip. We also really believed that she could not have physically made it day to day or enjoyed any of it.

For some unknown reason, a travel agent back in Virginia had suggested this trip for her, apparently having no idea what a "hiking" trip meant. Describing hiking trips to people who have never hiked much before is difficult. For 10 years I tried to accurately warn our customers planning to participate in organized 8-12 day trips around Mt. Adams in the Cascades of Washington state. My now ex-husband and I had designed, owned and operated a backpacking/climbing school attracting hopeful adventurers from all across the country. The 40-mile trip was strenuous, requiring carrying backpacks of 40-60 pounds and camping out, climbing up and down glaciers, and eating freeze-dried food every day of the trip.

Some clients came with new hiking boots still in the box, totally ignoring long explanations of how important it was to break in the boots ahead of time. Two New York City residents thought walking to (not around) Central Park from their apartment would be adequate to break in their boots. Here, likewise, Tillie had no idea of what she had signed up for. This was not for her.

Smoke finally tuned in to the problem. Encouraging the rest of us to go on to a halfway point, he walked back to Tillie for a heart-to-heart talk. We waited patiently, eventually hazarding guesses as to what the outcome might be. As time lengthened, our hope increased that perhaps she had been convinced of other options.

After ten years of running our backpacking school, I knew the inherent problems and real dangers of guiding the unfit. Even if her personality had been tolerable, I knew the trip would be infinitely smoother and more enjoyable for the rest of us without her. More to the point, she would have been miserable.

Time passed and finally we saw Smoke stepping lightly up the trail, with no Tillie in sight. "That was the easiest evacuation I've ever done!" He was perhaps more relieved than any of us, but he realized that she had had to make the decision to turn back herself, with some prodding, no doubt.

> Japan's hut system is a thing of beauty. We carried no sleeping bags, no food, and no cooking gear.

We started off again a bit more enthusiastically, though the clouds were warning us of sure rain. We had our lunch at our first midway hut. We bought Coke and hot noodles, symptomatic of the constant blending of East and West throughout Japan, put on our rain pants and headed up again. By 2:15 p.m. we arrived at the Ensanzo Hut, our first experience of a Japanese mountain hut. Without exaggeration, the very second we entered the door, a torrential rain slammed down outside. Our timing had been perfect.

And so was the hut, as were all the mountain huts we visited. Japan's hut system is a thing of beauty. We carried no sleeping bags, no food, and no cooking gear. The fact that clothes were the only things in my backpack allowed me to fit in my bagpipes. Because two of the three drones can be taken apart in sections, they can be stored compactly. Huts provided mattresses and clean bedding, food that varied from adequate to scrumptious, running water, and electricity.

These conveniences are mostly absent from the mountain huts I've used in the Colorado Rockies, though it appears that through the years, American huts are being updated and made more comfortable. The Japanese huts accommodated anywhere from a dozen or so travelers to hundreds of people.

One of the larger huts had piped-in classical music, beer and sake available, as well as video movies. I was to see first-hand one of the helicopters used to supply the huts with all the conveniences of home. While the clattering noise broke the mood of wilderness, I have to admit to enjoying the comforts.

Used to crawling into an undersized sagging tent, eating barely edible freeze-dried meals, and shivering all night in a lightweight sleeping bag, I found the Japanese hut system to be a welcome leap ahead of our own. Sure, it wasn't wild backcountry, self-sufficient stuff, but maybe this was an okay way to trek, too. Without the struggle of lugging a 50-pound pack all day, I found myself thoroughly enjoying the amenities.

The heavy rain lasted only an hour, but a serendipitous fog persisted. The sound of a bagpipe coming through fog has a magical quality to it and, in spite of hiding the view, the fog offered an ethereal setting for bagpipe playing outside the hut. Only two other Japanese hikers were using the hut that night. A younger, recently married couple doting on each other appreciated the music from a distance. This underscored a noticeable difference between the Japanese and Chinese cultures. The Japanese always maintained a polite distance whenever I was playing. It was a welcome relief from the intrusive crush felt from the Chinese.

After a nice dinner complete with sake, we sat down to enjoy the championship sumo wrestling on television. This was indeed a new way to hike. But, as they say, when in Japan, why not enjoy the Japanese ways? We all quickly found our favorite wrestler to cheer for in the matches.

Almost 20 years later, when I returned to Japan with an educators' group, I would be fortunate enough to see sumo wrestling up close at a championship match. There is a lot to learn about the Japanese ways by watching the tradition and concentration of sumo.

Smoke and I had hogged the conversation at dinnertime discovering mutual climbing friends and generally enjoying a common background for future comradeship. The others understandably lost interest.

I made an effort in the future to include all the participants in the conversation.

Breakfasts were served early; today's was at 5:30 a.m. And then we were off by 6:30 a.m. in a nippy nine degrees centigrade. We spent most of the day catching only glimpses of the surrounding high, pointy peaks. We ridge-walked through the mist and clouds, up and down, over fairly easy terrain. The path was obvious and contrasted nicely with the deep reds of the changing tundra flora of autumn.

Fall is my favorite season, perhaps because of all of the deep varying colors underfoot and surroundings. I followed Smoke, admiring his rock-solid balance and enjoyable pace. He continued last night's stories, fulfilling that part of a guide's duties with obvious glee. He reminded me of another famous mountaineer/explorer I had the good fortune to meet, Eric Shipton. Their experiences and successes in the mountains led them both to adopt a refreshing sense of humility.

Smoke emphasized the accomplishments of others, particularly one Norman Clyde, a Sierra climber as well. He also enjoyed sharing humorous stories about others. He recounted how Clyde had begun a backpack trip with 92 pounds on his back only to return six weeks later with 106 pounds! It seems he had added some stashed-away pots and pans he'd found along the way, as well as some food and fish he'd gathered. The tale rang of respect Smoke had for others. I found the same story in Smoke's book and realized he must have told some of these same stories hundreds of times.

Our lunch was taken at another midway hut just in time to enjoy a bit of sunshine. While relaxing with more hot noodles, we enjoyed the company of the resident Japanese family. We had come some five miles so far that day and were finally beginning to feel some warmth.

Smoke had been quick to see the possibilities of bagpipes in the Japanese Alps. I could see that he was excited to see what kind of reaction these Japanese would have to bagpipes and he requested a concert. Pulling them out of my pack, I struck up and played a quick tune.

A little girl about five years old was more demonstrative of her appreciation than the adults. But politeness was the ever-present demeanor of the Japanese. They stayed seated at their picnic table and tried hard not to stare—just the opposite of what the Chinese would have done. They applauded reservedly but seemed to enjoy the sound. I was reassured that I

Smoke Blanchard, our guide, and two clients enjoy
the skirl of the pipes.

would not have to endure the crowds and stares as I had
in China.

On the other hand, I was never to know for certain
whether the Japanese were just behaving politely or
if they, in fact, really liked the strange sounds. Tokyo
actually has its own bagpipe band, so the concept

may not have been entirely new to the locals. Having provided the musical entertainment for lunch, I tucked the pipes back into my pack, finished lunch, and headed for Nashidake Hut.

Not as well appointed as the other huts, this one still afforded welcome shelter from the rainstorm that again began minutes after we arrived. This would be the last rain we'd see until the final day in the mountains. But we would awaken to a thundering storm during the night, which did not bode well for our hike the next day. Miraculously, the skies cleared as we started hiking! Although this was in an area that has been known to pour on groups for 14 days straight, we never did hike while it was actually raining.

Our hiking times were not long, and next day's trek to Yarigadake Hut took only four-and-a-half hours. This time we encountered some steep elevation gain and loss. There was some impressive exposure that caused the heart to skip while looking straight down several hundred feet. Smoke said little about this added attraction and pressed on, thinking, no doubt, that the less said, the less imposing the dangers would appear.

I maintained that wonderful pace of his, marveling at his efficient motion. After settling in at the welcome hut, I spied Mt. Yari out the front door, and it screamed to be climbed. Yari has a rock peak that resembles a shark's tooth, looming a couple hundred feet above the hut. The route was complete with chains and ladders for the unsure hiker. Many of the group scrambled up in less than an hour. An impending typhoon that had threatened us for the past two days was nowhere in sight, and we enjoyed the spectacular 360 degree view.

While offering my bagpipe music to the gods on top, I appreciated the comparisons of these mountains to the Cascades of the American Northwest. Precipitous, rainy, expansive, both ranges are impressive. Also, at Yarigadake, I discerned some reserved appreciation for my music. But I was now definitely getting into a comfortable mood sharing bagpipe music with the Japanese.

Most Japanese throughout my visit seemed reluctant to use their English, though they study it in school from junior high on. They can be self-conscious because of the difficulties with their pronunciation.

This night we met three young Japanese fellows who were students actually eager to try their English with us. We committed a serious faux pas by introducing ourselves using our first names. The Japanese do not use their first names except with family. They were typically polite enough not to show their discomfort, but I realized our mistake too late. At least, we could ask questions about their country, which they were only too happy to answer. It seems that we Americans often need a lot of understanding and tolerance from the locals when we are visiting abroad.

The next morning we hiked down 3,000 feet into a river basin. A quick pipe practice by the river near our next hut was undisturbed by the many people nearby, and a long bath renewed my body. Again, I felt relief at being left alone for the afternoon.

Watching the Japanese hike in creased knickers, some even wearing white gloves, had made me self-conscious about my disheveled appearance. But there wasn't much I could do about it. Here, I was able to wash some clothes and enjoyed our tatami mats for sleeping. The comfort of the mat and comforter contrasted sharply with the rock hard pillow supplied in the inns. Filled with hard, uncooked rice, these pillows were not the comfy, soft things we have in the U.S. I'm not sure I could ever get used to them, but the Japanese grow up with them. The contrast between the soothing bath and the sumo wrestling we watched again that night also demonstrated the dichotomies in Japan.

Refreshed, we headed up again the next morning to the Karasawa Hut for a lunch of ... noodles, of course. This time we had the added treat of ice cream! I still found it strange but pleasant not to have to gorge myself with the ever-present gorp of nuts and chocolate for lunch that I would have when hiking at home. Hodaka Hut was in view 1,000 feet up the impressive ridge above us. Warm sunshine accompanied us, and with dozens of monkeys cavorting in the bushes alongside, we ascended the steep moraine.

Feeling particularly fit and energetic that afternoon and excited by the jagged peaks all around, I chugged up the last mile at a good clip and still had enough energy left over to play the pipes to encourage the others trudging up the last few hundred yards.

What I hadn't realized was that one of the flight attendants had a tendency to cry every time she heard bagpipes! As she approached me in front of the hut, I saw tears streaming down her face, and I became quite alarmed. Perhaps I really had been offending her with my playing. She assured me otherwise and, in fact, thanked me profusely for the inspiration I had provided with the pipe music for her last steps. Bagpipes just "moved" her, she said.

Again, there was a rocky, serrated peak, Hodaka, looming over the hut. Smoke and I clamored up the several hundred feet and enjoyed seeing mountains far to the horizon. He had made sure that I had brought my pipes to the top. I played to the peaks and the few Japanese also at the top.

When I finished the tune, we heard yells and noise from a group down below outside the hut. Had I gone too far and disturbed the tranquility of the Japanese Alps?

On top of a Japanese peak, I played to the crowd below at the hut.

A friendly Japanese man at the top set me straight and offered the information in English. He said they were yelling the equivalent of "encore" in Japanese! Surprised at such an overt reaction and pleased with the positive response, I complied and played another tune.

That night in the hut, fifty or so guests sat down to a tasty traditional Japanese dinner of pickled vegetables, soup, and various other dishes served, as always, in a very attractive, appealing manner. While we were eating, I felt an unexpected tap on my shoulder. "Were you the one playing bagpipes today?" came the inquiry in a very strong Scottish brogue. Scottish brogue?

I confirmed that I had been. He looked incredibly relieved. "I was hiking over here from another hut on the backside and heard the familiar sounds of home when I was some two miles away. I thought I was going daft. I couldn't imagine bagpipes in the mountains of Japan." He went on. "When I arrived, the sound had stopped, but I asked a hiker if he had seen someone playing a musical instrument. When he said yes and pointed you out, I was very relieved." I assured him he was not going daft, but that a crazy American female had decided to see what affect Scottish Highland bagpipes would have on the Japanese.

We talked for a bit, and I found out that he had been born and raised in Scotland and was teaching English in Japan for a year. He was burned out from teaching and was glad to be able to spend some time in these wonderful mountains. He hadn't had much of an opportunity to really see Japan.

We were to meet him again on our travels several days later at a different hut. He had taken a different route.

Smoke and I scrambled up the craggy peak on the other side of the hut the next morning. I played the pipes again, as our Scotsman hiked off into the distance.

The others, meanwhile, had descended back to the Karasawa Hut to spend a leisurely afternoon relaxing. Smoke and I enjoyed hiking without our group on the way down. As I absorbed the expansive view of soft-colored mountains and sucked in the fresh air, I remarked, "I can't think of anything else I'd rather be doing right now. This is perfect!"

At that moment, I looked down at my boot, which had suddenly felt a bit strange. The whole sole had ripped away from the leather. The boot had simply rotted apart! I then realized that my boots were fairly old and had had a lot of hard use in the past nine years. Why hadn't I thought to break in a new pair before heading for a Japanese hiking trip? I should have known better.

As I slowly comprehended the enormity of the crisis, Smoke had taken a roll of duct tape out of his pack. Without saying a thing, in stony silence, he threw it to me hoping I would figure something out. Without so much as a curse word and with resigned acceptance, I wrapped the tape around my boot, knowing it would not hold up for long. Not panicking yet or considering other options, I continued down the cirque to the hut. Smoke, on the other hand, could foresee the potential hazards. We had several days to go that would require good boots without which one could not take our planned route. He envisioned that I might have to be evacuated out of the mountains on a lower road.

The first thing he did on arriving at the hut was to ask the resident host about boots. Smoke had frequented this hut enough through the years that the host considered Smoke a good friend. Before I even removed my pack, I was presented with some boots left behind weeks before by some other luckless hiker who must have had other footwear. But these were no ordinary boots. The hut manager proffered red rubber, slick-soled boots two sizes too large for me.

In no position to be picky and look a gift horse in the mouth, I tried them on, wondering how they had come to even be called hiking boots in the first place. The slick sole was not what I was used to. Adding two extra pairs of socks would help with the fit. Looking down at the big bulbous toes, I accepted my gift with mustered gratitude. I just hoped that I wouldn't be tripping over my feet for the rest of the trip.

I repaid the hut manager's generosity with a bagpipe tune and consoled myself with a beer. His generosity knew no bounds, however. That night, my group was

seated separately from the other ten or so hikers at
the hut. One look at the table told us things would be
different for this dinner. A lettuce and tomato salad
greeted us instead of the omnipresent covered soup bowl.
Tonight, the hut manager was thanking Smoke for all the
business he had brought his way in the last decade.

Tonight, we would be served a Western style dinner.
While other hikers at the other table poked at rice and
pickled vegetables, we stared down with disbelief at real
Kobe beefsteak. We could literally cut it with a fork. The
massively thick piece of beef was as tender as veal and far
more flavorful.

Sadly the two vegetarians in our group couldn't
figure out how to show gratitude and still refrain from
eating the big chunks of steak. I managed to save our
collective face by eating one of the two other steaks as
well as my own. None of us felt very comfortable at
being singled out and treated so specially. But I, at least,
overcame my misgivings and voraciously devoured the
meal. I appreciated the typical Japanese dinners, but I
also appreciated the hutmeister's efforts at giving us a
special meal.

Generally, I found Japanese food to be very healthy and
enjoyable, as long as my stomach could identify what it
was. Some seafood did not sit well where other fish were

a treat. I learned to enjoy getting up from a meal feeling fully satisfied but not stuffed. Taking time to serve food in a pleasant arrangement has its rewards. In Japan, a pleasing appearance is almost as important as a good taste. And even in the huts, care was taken to have the food look good. The food had the unusual combination of looking good and having a delicious taste while actually being healthy at the same time.

The daily breakfast ritual of breaking a raw egg over hot rice, with the expectation that the egg would become cooked was one that I tired of. It never did cook! And I would end up eating a raw egg over rice. I learned this failure to actually eat cooked egg was partly because I had not learned the technique of digging a hollow in the rice for the egg.

I was to acquire appreciation for my boots the next day when we had a tough descent into the next valley over moraines, boulders, and down a wash. My old boots haphazardly duct-taped together never would have survived. When we reached Kamikuchi, a tourist area accessible by car, we had another opportunity at a bath and laundry.

Eager to return to the mountains the next day, I found this time the hike up was through rain forest, not my favorite eco-system. While I can appreciate the deep vegetation and myriads of bright greens, mauves and deepening shades of browns, I prefer the openness of high tundra. And the ever-present slippery roots grabbing at my feet at every step caused exasperation.

Our hut was at timberline. And, as everyone huddled in her own corner reading and writing, I decided to hike on up the ridge toward Hishiho Peak. Autumn was blowing across the ridge and a real chill settled in. I continued on, scrambling up and over rocky ledges and down crumbly precipices. With only a little exposure, I felt no real danger. But as I went on, I became aware that the ridge was one of those endless ones that led into the clouds. The scrambling was becoming more difficult, and I realized it was not wise to be alone in this situation.

I descended along with the falling temperature but felt very alive. As I neared the hut, against my better judgment because of the weather, I gave the pipes a shot. Rising wind and decreasing temperatures made the attempt unsuccessful and unsatisfying. My fingers and reeds decided not to work in harmony. The Scotsman who had shown up at the earlier hut was not impressed. Neither was I. I hustled into the warm hut with pipes safely tucked away in my pack.

The storm finally arrived in force and lasted all night. Heavy wind made the rain sting against the windows with a strident tone. Gust after gust seemed to shake the warmth out of the sturdy hut. Every half hour, I found myself looking at my watch.

If this rain kept up, I could see no way of negotiating the trail down the other side of the ridge. Steep gullies would be awash with rivulets and streams making nothing but mud to deal with. At 6:00 a.m., I detected a strange lack of noise. The storm had passed, and the wind had died down to a welcome breeze. Smoke showed no signs of worry and proceeded to pack up like normal.

The trail was indeed difficult to travel. Puddles thwarted direct descent. We were pushed off the trail into the thick bushes every 20 yards. The mud was like oozy oil, carrying us down the trail farther and faster than desired. Grabbing branches and whole trees to attain some control usually met with a handful of leaves and a wet face. My rubber boots weren't so bad now after all! We slipped our mud-soaked bodies down and down until we finally emerged from the dank, drippy forest at 3:00 p.m.

Nakoa Hot Springs was a paradise after our ordeal. And the requisite soaping and rinsing before the bath was never so needed. Our *ryokan* had the added attraction of an outdoor, rocked-in hot springs pool to soak in. After several cups of sake, we all felt comfortable enough to submerge ourselves in the nude.

Few baths in Japan are co-ed. But this one entertained anyone who was willing to step from the separate washrooms outside to the delightful pool. I'm sure that Smoke didn't mind. Fortunately, the six of us were the only visitors enjoying the exquisite setting of that hot springs that evening.

> Mindfulness, lack of ego, acceptance, and "being present" are all ingrained in everyday life in Japan.

Our meal that night was commensurate with the setting. Tasty, attractive, and wholly pleasurable, the dinner was superb. Kneeling on cushions in our *yukata* robes at a low table, we had become accomplished with chopsticks and proper manners. We never left our chopsticks sticking into the bowl. This is considered an insult and only done for cremations. Our robes were folded right over left, not left over right, as corpses are dressed. But I could never last the entire meal on my knees; I always found myself slouching one way or another by the end of dinner. My knees just hadn't been properly trained.

Many years later, I would explore Buddhism and sit endlessly in meditation. Even then I had to master my own technique with the zafu or meditation pillow to last for a sitting of 40 minutes.

I only wish I had immersed myself with Buddhism before my two trips to Japan. My impression was that the whole of Japanese culture and way of life reflects Buddhism and its tenets. Mindfulness, lack of ego, acceptance, and "being present" are all ingrained in everyday life in Japan. And a deeper understanding of this would have increased my appreciation of what I was seeing and enjoying in Japan. Obviously, I would not be playing my pipes during meditation. The more formal approach to such things in Japan contrasted with the Chinese invitation to play during their tai chi.

13

THE OTHER JAPAN

At first, I figured this was some kind of joke. The longer I looked, the more I realized this was for real—a Japanese pub called "The Bagpipe." In English letters, plain and simple, the word was unmistakable.

Our hiking in Japan was over. I thought that hiking in the United States would be clouded forevermore. Where are the huts that serve wonderful meals with clean bedding and classical music? The Appalachian Trail system in the East supports some nice huts. The Tenth Mountain Hut system in Colorado provides for atmospheric huts that are consistently being updated for cross-country skiers as well as hikers.

However, we have not developed the hut idea to the degree and quality the Japanese have. We may be moving in that direction slowly. But perhaps we don't want huts everywhere that need to be supplied by noisy helicopters interrupting the stillness of the wilderness. Still, I'd go hiking in Japan again in a heartbeat, though I still very much enjoy hiking in our own mountains.

Cleaned and cleansed, physically and psychically, we boarded a bus to Takayama, a popular tourist destination. The site of a unique festival in spring, Takayama is full of meandering streets filled with no end of items for tourists to buy. A museum of restored seventeenth century buildings highlights the town. Grass-thatched roofs a good foot or more in thickness easily shed the downpour I experienced during my leisurely walk through the old town.

The same peace and quietude I had found in the mountains followed me along the paths of the town-museum. Exactly how this sensation is created is elusive. I experienced this feeling whenever I stepped through a threshold of a Japanese inn. The outer world disappeared behind me.

As I parked my shoes on the entry step and eased into my slippers in the lovely *ryokan* of Takayama, my crunched, tense shoulders relaxed. Retreating into a private tatami room with the ever-present cup of tea readily made from the service on the low table, I was wondering how I could recreate this atmosphere back home.

I walked continuously from 11 a.m. to 6 p.m. through the charming streets of Takayama. I must admit to feeling a bit more civilized in "city" clothes as opposed to the ripe hiking garb I had in the mountains. I had no heavy boots to impede my progress or pipes on my back to add to the discomfort in my shoulders.

Rounding one of the many corners I had taken that afternoon, I stopped mid-stride at the unbelievable sight before me, with the proverbially dropped jaw. At first, I figured this was some kind of joke. The longer I looked, the more I realized this was for real—a Japanese pub called "The Bagpipe." In English letters, plain and simple, the word was unmistakable.

After standing unmoving for several minutes trying to accept what I was seeing was real, I cautiously entered. My expectations were difficult to restrain. Fortunately, these had had little time to blossom. No one was inside, save a few lonely non-English-speaking Japanese. After ordering some tea, I tried to discover the reason for the name. There were some British touches to the friendly tavern— the half-timbered look inside and out, the colored glass windows. But basically, it was still just a typical Japanese business. I saw one photograph of a bagpipe hanging forlornly on the wall.

I tried to communicate with the reticent waitress. She wanted no part of an intense American visitor who kept throwing unintelligible questions at her. Repeated inquiries about the owner were met with shakes of the head and equally unintelligible Japanese responses. I think, but I'm not sure, I succeeded in conveying the fact that I played the bagpipes.

The idea of playing the pipes at a pub called The Bagpipe in Takayama, Japan, was too delicious to comprehend. Of course, this was a time when I'd left the pipes back at our lodging! Without anyone else patronizing the place, even if I had them along, playing the pipes wouldn't have been too exciting. Perhaps, at least, I could have had a photograph for the record.

Feeling totally deflated, I walked out; there was nothing else to do. We would leave Takayama the next day before The Bagpipe opened, and I would have no chance to return with pipes in hand. I surmised that the owner may have spent some time in Scotland and brought back some of the old country in the form of the pub. Or perhaps it was owned by an ex-pat from Scotland who couldn't leave everything of the old country behind. What a good time we could have had if he'd been present. The world is full of lost opportunities.

Our stay in Kyoto was pleasant, if not a bit unsettling. Smoke had arranged for us to stay at the Myoshin-ji Temple on the outskirts of the city. In the large Buddhist complex, one small, insignificant building housed visitors expecting simplicity and quiet. We quickly named our hostess Dragon Lady for her constant unpleasant visage. She seemed very unhappy to have us there. We were unceremoniously shown a tatami room which opened onto a lovely garden.

The fare was basic but good, and opportunities to view Buddhism in practice were abundant. I am only sorry that my immersion in Buddhism came many years later. I was not in a position to adequately appreciate the setting of a Buddhist temple at that point in my life. I would spend a day and night at a Buddhist Temple in 2005 when I returned to Japan, but, again, that is hardly a taste of what Buddhism offers.

The contrast between a strenuous many-day hike and the quiet of a Buddhist Temple was jarring. The 9:00 p.m. curfew was not attractive to the five of us who wanted to experience a bit of Kyoto's nightlife. The three flight attendants were first with the idea of checking out of our temple and into a downtown hotel.

My roommate and I followed suit, though we went to different lodging. They wanted some luxury; we wanted some flavor of Japan and stumbled into a *ryokan* near the train station. Here again, even though we were in the middle of the daily rush of downtown, our inn immediately offered a sense of peace and quiet upon entering.

Mary and I spent the next day traveling about the town from garden to temple to garden. One could spend weeks visiting the gardens of Kyoto. My pipes all but forgotten, I enjoyed the big city in spite of its noise and fast pace.

After another day of touring outside town, I decided to return to the temple, partly in deference to Smoke and partly due to a desire to experience more of the uniqueness of the Buddhist surroundings. There was only a little temptation to disrupt the flow of Buddhist calmness with a bagpipe concert. I refrained without much difficulty and enjoyed walking the grounds.

All of us rendezvoused the next day at the train station for the quick trip back to Tokyo. The last night would be spent having dinner with Smoke and Keiko, his girlfriend, at a very nice local restaurant. Smoke had made it very clear, and would brook no reluctance on my part, that I was to bring my bagpipes with me. He couldn't wait to show my pipes and me off to Keiko.

After dinner, we wandered to a central park of some sort in Tokyo, if there is such a thing. I never did get much of a sense of a "downtown." The city is comprised of neighborhoods that grew together over the centuries. But we were among a few high-rises and near some big name hotels. It was in the outdoor courtyard of one of these buildings that Smoke determined I should play.

I complied and was relieved that there weren't many people in the area. After a tune, Smoke threw some coins in a hat he had laid out near me. A Japanese fellow, probably trying to impress his good-looking date, also threw in some coins. I managed to gather enough for a beer. Smoke and Keiko were satisfied, and we went into a restaurant for some dessert.

As I boarded the plane for home, my mind was overwhelmed with the events of the past two months. I wasn't even too thrilled about returning home. I regret not following my desire to arrange a trip on the Trans-Siberian Railroad. There wasn't anything in particular to come back to. I would be housesitting for a few months, substitute teaching, and working at the sports store again and still at loose ends. But events were in motion, and I was on the plane back to Denver.

I wouldn't see Smoke again, though I hoped to at some time, perhaps on a trip to California where he spent part of the year. Many months after the trip, I was to hear of his death in a bizarre car accident in Bishop, California. It seemed a poor way for him to go. I expected to hear of him walking into the mountains and disappearing. At least this vibrant man would not suffer some affliction that would make him an armchair mountaineer. I wanted to play my pipes at his memorial but could not make the necessary arrangements. I think he would have liked that.

14

PIED PIPER OF PATAGONIA

The huasos, also known as gauchos or South American cowboys, were very appealing with their flat-brimmed black hats, weather-beaten ponchos, sheepskin chaps, wooden stirrups and, best of all, huge silver spurs. Their faces had the look that all "cowboys" should have, tanned and creased from the wind. They knew the land and the outdoors, and it was theirs.

P atagonia! This word produced as much consternation with others as did my bagpipe playing. Not only did people ask me why I had learned to play the bagpipes, but now they also asked me why I was going to Patagonia, or, in some cases, they asked where it was.

Many know that Patagonia refers to a line of outdoor wear. Working at Eastern Mountain Sports, the "outdoor specialists" in Boulder, for more than two years had taught me that Patagonia "pile" jackets were a necessary accoutrement of any outdoor jock worth his salt. Now I was headed for its namesake, the tip of South America.

Patagonia is home to some of the most impressive climbing tales of the 20th and 21st century. Eric Shipton, mentioned previously, the great English explorer and reconnoiterer of Mt. Everest, did some of his most incredible exploits on the Southern Ice Cap of Chile. His incomparable feat of negotiating the entire length of the Southern Ice Cap in 1960 had never been duplicated, at least up through 1988, when I experienced Patagonia.

Mt. Fitzroy has produced mind-boggling tales of boulders hurtling through the night at precariously perched climbers, only to be lifted miraculously upward just in time by gale force winds in the area, sparing the climbers' sure death. Whether these are entirely tall tales or have a grain of truth in them, they add to the myriad of controversies in the climbing community regarding climbs, or almost climbs, or who climbed what first.

Even popular author, Paul Theroux, wrote about traveling throughout South America in *The Old Patagonia Express*. He reached Patagonia by train only in the last chapter and was none too complimentary, but Patagonia has become known to people who have wanderlust in their hearts.

Telling friends and relatives that I was going to southern Chile and Argentina didn't have the same romantic ring as beguiling them with the word "Patagonia." I waited until halfway through my trip before I wondered how the name Patagonia originated.

In the 1800s, Chile had been the proud owner of all the southern tip of South America. Argentina pressed for her share of this area at the opportune time—on the heels of a war Chile had just fought with Peru. Some otherwise inconsequential bureaucrat decided there was nothing to be lost by ceding this part of the world to Argentina. Thus, as in many far-reaching, great historical moments, borders were changed in the late 1800s and early 1900s that, to this day, produce antagonisms unforeseen at the time.

Patagonia refers to the whole of the southern part of South America from Rio Negro, 40 degrees south, to the Straits of Magellan, a distance of 1,000 miles. Sometimes Patagonia is referred to as "Land of the Giants."

However, this is an incorrect description of the Indians by Magellan's men. Magellan, a Portuguese explorer who circumnavigated the Earth in the early 1500s, had first used the term "Patagonia" or "big feet" resulting from seeing men so tall that "others came up to their midriff."

Darwin collaborated the great size of the "Patagons," though probably at 6 feet instead of the implied 8 feet average. "Pata" does mean foot or hoof in Spanish, but "gon" is meaningless according to Bruce Chatwin in *Patagonia Revisited*. He mentions a Patagon in a 1512 book called *Primaleon of Greece*, a book Magellan could easily have read.

I left Denver on a clear, sunny February day. Why was I leaving the powder slopes of Steamboat Springs, Winter Park, or Snowmass ski areas to head toward a poor excuse for summer in the Southern Hemisphere? The best skiing of the season was beckoning me to test my new skis. If I ever succumbed to the lure of steady employment in the future, I would have to become one of the mad weekend skiers despairing at packed parking lots, suffering winding lift lines, traffic jams on the highways, and a half an hour wait to spend a minor fortune for a basic lunch. This year, because of my intermittent employment, I had the opportunity to ski at will during the mid-week quiet. And I was leaving all this to head for the unknown!

But this was just the very reason I was going at this time. If I were to obtain a teaching job, I would not have Februarys or Marches to experience touring during the upside down season in the South. Dire tales of hideous weather abounded regarding Patagonia, even in summer. But its winter was not inviting for someone who wanted to travel about at will, without fighting blizzards at every turn. I could go to Europe, Russia, Japan, and Canada, even Africa during a teacher's summer vacation, but not Patagonia.

Patagonia was different. I had to go now, during my winter, to enjoy anything resembling its summer. Besides, not many of the Chileans, or Chilanos, as they call themselves, knew what bagpipes sounded like, or so I thought.

My first taste of South America greeted me in Miami Airport. I heard more Spanish than English. I wished I had taken one of those Spanish language courses for tourists. My misfortune was to arrive at 4:00 p.m. on a Friday with all the suburban yuppies grappling for supposed rest and relaxation through cruise line tour operators. Noise and mayhem were everywhere, as were anxious faces hoping their wads of money would buy some form of peace—or at least a tan to parade back at the office. Ah, what an impact a set of good-sounding bagpipes would have had in front of the Eastern Airlines counter!

Because of all the fun experiences I had of playing bagpipes to the uninitiated of China and Japan, I had to take them with me to Chile! But Eastern Airlines was spared that day.

> So I crammed into a booth at a bar in the airport, bagpipes poking their drones out of my daypack, telling me they wanted none of this airport world.

Prospects of a six-hour layover and an eight-hour flight dampened any enthusiasm for disrupting the flow of traffic with a bagpipe tune in the Miami Airport. I am not a good flyer and rely on "Dutch courage," trusting to a little gin and tonic to see me through long flights. The wise and worldly traveler knows that booze only complicates jet lag. But since Santiago, Chile, was close to the same meridian as New York City, I foresaw no great time changes. Travel time from Denver to Santiago turns out to be only a four-hour difference. Santiago's time was ahead of Denver's!

So I crammed into a booth at a bar in the airport, bagpipes poking their drones out of my daypack, telling me they wanted none of this airport world. I paced my alcohol intake to no more than enough to induce sleepiness for the flight and wearily trudged onto the plane after 11 p.m. I was ready to cope with trying to sleep through the night on board as well as a new culture when I arrived.

As the plane descended into Santiago, I contemplated all the ramifications of modern-day jet travel. Here I was at the other end of the Earth in less than a day! I hope I never lose that sense of incredulity toward the compression of space that the jet-age has wrought. I find it difficult to keep a good perspective on how far away from home I am in miles when only a short time is needed to travel there. I had come more than 5,000 miles into another country and culture and had had less than a total of 20 or so hours to prepare and adjust.

Perhaps that is one reason so many Americans have such a difficult time accepting the fact that other countries are not managed like the United States.

"Americans" is a term not totally appropriate when loosely given to citizens of the United States. The Chilanos are also Americans, i.e. residents of South America as the Canadians are residents of North America. Both groups could be considered "Americans." But, for convenience, I'll use "Americans" to refer to those living in the United States.

Americans rush into Spain, Slovakia, Tanzania, Japan and places rarely heard of only to face a new cultural world as soon as they step off of the plane. The culture shock was truer in 1988 when I visited Chile than it is now. Today I have trouble being in an airport anywhere in the world without seeing a Starbuck's as soon as I enter the terminal! One minute these people are in O'Hare Airport in Chicago fighting the familiar delays and crowds waiting for yesterday's plane. Then they find themselves in, say, Kathmandu, Nepal, wondering where the luggage claim is.

Disembarking in Santiago, many tourists face a new language and, in the late 1980s, a lack of fully mechanized and sterilized movers of luggage as well as different people. These inconveniences can cause immediate anxiety to the uninitiated and insecure. American tourists can feel backed into an unfamiliar defensive role. And thus the "Ugly American" is born. With the advent of more frequent traveling by Americans as well as the rest of the world, along with the modernization and globalization of the world, these situations are becoming less and less common.

Still, I saw a wild-eyed false sense of brashness cross the faces of several of my fellow travelers. Here we go again. Would I never learn that traveling with a group had its pitfalls? My group consisted of 10 to 12 other Americans who had thrown money at a travel organization hoping to remove some of the hassles of travel. They were all somewhat well seasoned travelers, at least in mileage. The accumulative miles everyone had traveled were in the millions. And their destinations had been exotic. More than one had been to Antarctica. Several had been all around Africa, Nepal, and Tibet, not to mention Australia and Europe.

Money was no problem to any of these people, save for Cathy, a 40-year-old fellow substitute teacher from California, and myself. She and I quickly became comrades-in-arms, forming a bulwark against the remaining group of mostly 60+ year olds.

The group would have made a good model for characters in a television sitcom. One couple thought talking to each other consisted of only nagging, yelling, criticizing or generally berating the other. Incredibly, they had no idea they were constantly carping at each other. They were impervious to their own arguments, which disturbed the tranquility of the trip for the rest of us. The better half of the pair was a German lady who was not wanting in assertiveness. This wiry, curly-headed ball of energy proved to be an entertaining foil for her husband's barbs.

"You should have some tea, Tony. It's good for the digestive system."

"But I hate tea; I've never liked tea. Why do you always tell me to have some tea when I never have wanted any? After 20 years of marriage, you should remember I hate tea."

"But really, Tony, it's good for you. Have some."

And so on, back and forth, neither giving an inch.

And so it went. Or, perhaps he was a foil for her? At first it was amusing, but all this squabbling proved wearing. As it happened, both would feel the effects of "tourista," which solved the problem for a few days while they retreated to their rooms to nurse their queasy stomachs.

These weren't the only two who tried the patience of the rest of the group. I practiced the art of transferring my feeling of anger to that of contemplation, asking why Mabel and Harry chose to travel at all. They were opposites but shared the contemptible traits of being overly critical and demanding. Traveling as singles, their rooms were never right—either they weren't singles, or they were single but too far from the rest of the group, or they were too small.

Where Mabel constantly blurted out inane questions of all kinds that demanded detailed answers such as, "What is that house over there?" Harry showed no curiosity whatsoever. I decided I would waste no more energy trying to engage in friendly conversation with him after a comment he later made at the base of Mt. Fitzroy.

A splinter group had donned hiking boots for a five-hour hike to the base of one of the most famous peaks in Patagonia, if not the world. We reached the objective and witnessed one of the most awesome views anywhere, looking up at this abrupt granite face of many thousand feet. Harry's single comment, when asked what he thought, was, "Pretty cold."

Mabel and Harry never ceased making demands. Mabel insisted on stopping at every corner for a "photo opportunity," regardless of what anyone else wanted. Not so alarming in itself, indeed, even appreciated from time to time, these stops piled on top of each other. Even if she was the only one wanting to take a picture, she was completely unaware of any inconvenience she caused others.

One incident is engraved in my memory forever. Our bus slowed for a small cattle drive passing on our one lane gravel road. The *huasos*, also known as gauchos or South American cowboys, were very appealing with their flat, straight-brimmed black hats, weather-beaten ponchos, sheepskin chaps, wooden stirrups and, best of all, huge silver spurs. Their faces had the look that all "cowboys" should have, tanned and creased from sun and wind. They knew the land and the outdoors, and it was theirs.

Even with a small tour bus complicating their progress, they were accommodating to the tourists and stopped so that we could take their photos. Two on horseback had passed us only to stop 50 yards down the road, either to allow us a photo, or, I thought, to give us all another look-over. We presented as strange a sight to them as they did to us.

The apparition that approached them didn't disappoint any expectations of weird behavior. Mabel, with her tiny instamatic camera, came wallowing toward them, all 200-plus pounds of her in her bright blue, floral-patterned mumu. She had finally realized that she had to be close for her photos to have any chance of resembling the actual subject. What these two *huasos* thought as she lumbered closer and closer, I cannot imagine. I can only hope that their impression of Americans was not based on this encounter alone.

Two fellows from Seattle joined our group. One, the only other member of our group under 60 years old besides Cathy and myself, was an architect on his first group travel experience. His friend was a soft-spoken retired Boeing engineer whose whole life now involved traveling. His sense of humor saved me on many occasions.

My roommate was also a world-traveler from Chicago who became known as "Mama Sue" because if anyone needed anything from pharmaceuticals to shower clips to extra camera batteries, she had it. Sharon has drifted away in my memory. A nice but somewhat mousey housewife from Virginia, she had traveled some but showed few signs of having gained good perspectives on life because of these experiences. She had traveled everywhere but perhaps really nowhere.

Three other couples completed the entourage. Except for one gentleman who had been a professor of music at Chico State University and showed great interest in my bagpipes, the rest have faded into dull shadows. They were agreeable enough traveling companions, but none of us pretended to have much in common except for an interest in Patagonia. And after the 3,680 miles of driving we endured down the spine of Chile, including our side trips, we needed more than the vague interest in Chile to maintain our equanimity. We retreated into our own thoughts. Even Cathy became more intrigued with her bird watching as the trip progressed.

So this was the group I would spend 25 days in Chile and Argentina with. After my trips to China and Japan, I vowed I would never sign up for a group trip again. After all, Chile would not be as difficult as China to negotiate alone. I thought I could manage, even though my Spanish was non-existent. I had traveled alone throughout the United States, Europe and Mexico. I was confident I could do it again.

I chose not to. One of the more delightful parts of traveling is sharing the thoughts and experiences with fellow travelers. I decided to risk encountering the bad apples always found in such groups.

> A common thread to some American travelers abroad is their inability, or unwillingness, to listen.

I know myself well enough to know of my capabilities of ignoring obnoxious behaviors. After all, at that time I had taught elementary and high school for 12 years! If the bad apples weren't too bad, I could overlook dumb comments for as much as a month. Really distasteful stuff cuts the tolerance time to two weeks. That's about when patience starts to wear thin, and did so on this trip. Perhaps it was the fact that there were two bad apples this time, or perhaps it was because they were so vociferous in their demands. Whichever it was, I found myself practicing my chanter on the bus more and more to drown out their noises. Now who was the bad apple?

A common thread to some American travelers abroad is their inability, or unwillingness, to listen. I heard more about what the United States was like from our group than I heard conversations about where we were. What a wasted opportunity! Here was a chance to learn in living color what Chilanos thought and how they lived.

Perhaps the sense of self-absorption is due to an all-encompassing feeling of superiority. I've always valued and found that some humility can create an atmosphere for more learning. I was hoping to see more courtesy and curiosity toward another culture. I was to travel with other groups that did, indeed, demonstrate these qualities. The difference may be, as I mentioned earlier, just the luck of the draw with specific groups.

In all fairness to the group as a whole, I have to say I appreciated their forbearance with my bagpiping. To a person, they indicated they enjoyed hearing it whenever I chose to bring the pipes out. In fact, bagpipe tunes became a real morale booster at certain tense or otherwise lagging times. If only one of them had objected, I would have changed my approach to my playing.

A world champion piper claimed he was quoting the Library of Congress when he said that bagpipes are the second most popular instrument in the U.S. Just what is meant by popular, he didn't say! Whether or not this statement is accurate, hyperbole, or just wishful thinking, is not really important. He did point to the fact that there were no piano bands as there are bagpipe bands!

I have found in my personal experiences of playing in various environments, most people do enjoy listening to bagpipes. However, there are an errant few who intensely dislike the bagpipes. Therefore, I find it difficult to impose the sound on those who cover their ears while I play. I have heard there actually may be a physical cause for this intolerance for the sound. But the enjoyment of playing is understandably lost in those situations. This group, again, was a receptive audience, and I did appreciate that.

None of the group knew anything about bagpipes, and I could make mistakes without being self-conscious. The exception was the music professor who had perfect pitch and knew when I was even slightly out of tune. Unfortunately for him, this was just about all the time. Bless his heart, he never tired of helping me to tune. The changing climate and altitude wreaked havoc on my reeds. I was more interested in practicing and didn't always have the time or desire to carefully tune. Fellow pipers will cringe at such an admission, but one renowned world-class piper recorded one of his practice sessions and found he spent fully three-fourths of his practice time just tuning. He adjusted and decreased significantly just how much tuning he did from then on. The truth is I am not a perfectionist, which made piping easier for me.

15

NOT A GOOD START IN SANTIAGO

As I took my pipes out of my daypack, a fellow not far away began whistling, "Scotland the Brave," the tune identified with Scottish bagpipes and probably the most famous pipe tune of all. I was surprised at the rapidity of his response after seeing the pipes, even in Santiago, Chile.

I try to avoid relying on first impressions of people, and I was unaware of just what the group would be like when we arrived in downtown Santiago, my pipes tucked away in my well-used daypack. I took one look at the luxurious Carrera Hotel and realized that my first piping would not be in this lobby. This was first class stuff and foreshadowed the cosmopolitan flavor we would experience in Santiago.

The only way to really "see" a city, I had learned in China, was on foot. So off I went with vague directions toward the center of the city. This was Chile's summer and everyone was out walking. As I approached the shopping streets, I immediately was struck by the casual ambiance of the Chilanos. These people were warm, open, and, most importantly, unafraid. Given their recent political upheavals during and following Salvador Allende's rule, I had a difficult time understanding this phenomenon. Why should they be so open? Either they were relishing their newfound relative security, and/or their history had created a special outlook on life.

The Spanish started settling in Chile in 1511. Jose F. de San Martìn along with a Bernardo O'Higgins (yes, O'Higgins!) drove the Spanish rulers out in 1817. The O'Higgins name is seen everywhere, from street signs to buildings. The one million Indians that met the Spaniards, as in so many places, mixed and intermarried with the Spaniards as well as with some German, English, and Irish settlers to produce the nine million mestizos today. However, the Araucanian Indians resisted and fought on for three centuries!

Chile was truly a mixture. My Irish ancestry was attracted to the O'Higgins name and saw a kindred spirit of independence. And then there was the Royal Guard beer, which Chile had to import from England. It turns out that Chile makes great wine but poor beer.

So the Chilanos enjoy uniqueness in this world, with its mixture of peoples and in its geography and geology. Only in 1988 had the country been united by the so-called "Pan-American Highway." A closer look at the highway at that time revealed that it was neither a highway as we often envision one, nor did it totally connect Santiago to Punta Arenas on the Straits of Magellan as advertised in the adventure trip operator's brochure.

The road from Puerto Montt, 640 miles south of Santiago, where we actually started our journey to Punta Arenas, was only somewhat better than a one-lane gravel track. A lack of bridges over the myriad rivers demanded the use of short ferry rides here and there. However quaint and endearing these ferries were, the lack of a modern advanced transportation system had resulted in an independent attitude of the locals in the various regions of Chile. Combined with the severe weather conditions, the remoteness of certain areas has caused the people to have a strong sense of self-reliance.

The Andes basically run the entire length of the country, reaching closer and closer to the sea the farther south they extend. I was surprised at the amount of agriculture stuck in between these grand mountains and the ocean. Since the great grape disaster of 1989, when a small amount of cyanide was found in two grapes and Chilean grapes were withdrawn from all the American supermarkets, the world has become aware of Chile's important fruit harvest. In fact, Chilean wine has since gained a very good reputation.

The Chilanos live with a daily threat of earthquakes that rattle so frequently that small ones elicit little or no attention, and conversations proceed as if the lamps weren't really shaking. Perhaps, again, it is the remoteness of the country from the rest of the world, or perhaps it is the rugged environment that creates the pleasant demeanor of the Chilanos. Whatever it is, I thoroughly enjoyed the Chilean people.

My introduction to these attitudes began in the central plaza of Santiago. The atmosphere was reminiscent of what I see today on the Pearl Street Mall in Boulder, Colorado, only more relaxed and genuine here. People were ambling along enjoying the evening as the small groups of entertainers set themselves up in the plaza. *Huaso* dancers and singers were particularly popular as are magicians and guitarists in Boulder. Playing to the pedestrian traffic can be seen as an ignominious way to earn money, but hats were passed and money was being made.

I didn't take too long to realize that here was my opportunity to see what the Chilanos thought of the bagpipes. I had even read in one of the many tour guides that, of the many activities to be seen in the Plaza des Armes, even a bagpiper could be heard! So, I wouldn't be the first. Perhaps that was just as well.

Revving up my courage, I returned to the hotel to gather my bagpipes and to recruit Cathy as my photographer. The familiar butterflies began forming in my stomach the closer we got to the plaza. This was not going to be a situation where I could melt into the crowd if I felt uncomfortable. It was becoming clear to me that once I began playing, I would be the focus of attention of more than just a few of the Santiago residents.

My walk slowed perceptibly as we reached the point of no return. I discerned one method to save face while sidestepping my initial brave desire to play. I saw a policeman and figured it would be a good idea to ask his permission to play. A lack of common language produced a lot of hand signals but basically no communication. I gave up on the attempt and proceeded across the plaza to a less crowded area, not sure of my situation at all. What had seemed like a good idea suddenly appeared to be just plain foolish.

Nevertheless, I was committed and was truly curious to see the reaction from the Chilanos. Cathy positioned herself to get a good quick photo in case I felt the need to stop short. As I took my pipes out of my daypack, a fellow not far away began whistling, "Scotland the Brave," the tune identified with Scottish bagpipes and probably the most famous pipe tune of all. I was surprised at the rapidity of his response after seeing the pipes, even in Santiago, Chile.

> I had brought my pipes to Patagonia, as I had done in China and Japan, foremost for practicing purposes. After my experiences in those two countries, I was prepared to do my part to introduce the sound of the pipes to the Chilanos.

Before I had my pipes put together, a small crowd of 30-50 curious onlookers was already gathering. Time to tune properly was out of the question. In my haste to put everything together, one of my drone reeds fell into the bag, a not altogether totally uncommon occurrence with pipers. Without it in its place, I couldn't maintain enough air in the bag to get any sound; the air would rush out of the reedless drone. In another less tense situation, I would feel for the reed on the outside of the bag. There's no opening large enough to put your fingers inside the bag to grasp the errant reed. I quickly put a cork in the end of the drone, cutting off air outtake and made a perfunctory effort to get at least two drones in tune.

With a throng quickly gathering, off I went into an easy tune I knew by heart. Already there were more people staring at me than I was accustomed to. What had I thought would happen? I guess I had tried not to make too many predictions; otherwise I'd have chickened out from the first. For as many times as I was doing this sort of thing, I had not become totally accustomed to any of it.

I had brought my pipes to Patagonia, as I had done in China and Japan, foremost for practicing purposes. After my experiences in those two countries, I was prepared to do my part to introduce the sound of the pipes to the Chilanos.

Introducing different cultures to others was a heady trip. But this experience in Santiago's city center was a little more than I bargained for. After a tune or two, I stopped to ask if Cathy had succeeded in her photographic duties. After all, for all my discomfort,

I'd better end up with at least a good photograph.
As she nodded yes, I was gestured to play more by the
enthusiastic audience. I complied, starting to get with the
flow of the scene. It was about that time I saw the same
policeman I had tried in engage in conversation stick his
head into the crowd and nudge Cathy.

I made eye contact with him, as he quietly shook his
head "no," and wagged a finger back and forth at me.
I finished the tune and was actually relieved to have
an excuse to pack up. I was a bit chagrined, though
not surprised. The reaction of the Santiaguinos is what
surprised me. As the policeman retreated to the street,
they started whistling and booing at the policeman's
actions! I have to admit to feeling a bit vindicated.

The bulk of the spectators then swelled in next to me as
I was pulling the drones apart to fit into my daypack, and
they rattled questions off in Spanish. I didn't have the skill
to understand or reply and hastily beat a retreat back to
the hotel. Cathy and I consoled ourselves by sipping pisco
sours next to the rooftop swimming pool and wondered
why others could perform on the plaza but I could not.
Thoughts of racism or nationalism didn't wash.

Two weeks later, a plausible answer surfaced. The
Seattle fellows in our group said they had witnessed the
affair from a nearby park bench. Our group really hadn't

introduced themselves to each other yet, and they were unsure as to whether or not I was a part of their group at the time. They had noticed that the policeman pointed to the grass and then over across the way. Sign language didn't go far enough. Cathy thought the policeman figured we were selling marijuana—known as grass.

In fact, according to my fellow travelers, he wanted me to play where the crowd could stand on cement and not the grass. All he wanted me to do was to move to a paved area! I trusted that my future pipe-playing experiences in Chile would improve.

I didn't play again in Santiago. We had only two days there, and I wanted to just enjoy the atmosphere unencumbered without bagpipes drawing attention to myself. I wanted to be the viewer, not the viewed.

From the perch on top of our hotel, we cast our eyes over the city. We realized we were in one of the highest buildings of Santiago—16 or 17 stories. Of course, Santiago would be a "low" city. The frequent earthquakes are not kind to tall buildings unless you're in a location such as Japan. The Japanese have such a huge population density, they have designed skyscrapers that sway but don't "break" during earthquakes. I understand that modern Santiago is changing its skyline to include skyscrapers. I trust they sway.

Slowly, I realized that the clouds I'd been gazing at in the distance were snow-covered peaks! Santiago rests in a basin surrounded by mountains. While adding beauty to the skyline, the topography unfortunately, also traps the pollution from the cars. Haze is an ever-present companion to the people of Santiago. I was lucky to have seen the mountains at all, many miles in the distance.

The city itself was an odd mixture of architecture of solid concrete government buildings but also displayed Spanish influence of ornately carved wooden doors. Parks were numerous and lent greenery as a contrast to the drab gray concrete background. Houses were variously British, French, or German inspired; the half-timbered British, French mansards, or Tyrolean influences are evident. I wondered what was Chilean. In fact, the entire combination was Chilean, a confluence of European and native influences.

16

HEADING SOUTH TO SOUTH

These particular children spoke no English but quietly sat down next to me and listened politely and clapped when I finished. I figured that sign language was needed to complete the cycle. I held my hands to my ears and they laughed. Some barrier had been broken, and I felt totally comfortable in Chile from that day on.

On our last day in Santiago, we finally met Manuel who would be our guide for the trip. In eight days we would meet Pablo, the official leader. Whether it was because of Manuel's personality or his longer stay with us, I couldn't tell, but he was the more personable of the two and seemed to epitomize and personify the amiable Chilean attitude and personality. His attitude toward life was nothing but positive and admirable. He truly lived one day at a time. Nothing rattled him, and everything interested him. His understatements were studied. They belied and, at the same time, gave credence to his appreciation for life.

"Manuel," I asked, as we approached an unnamed cave, "what is it about this cave that makes it worthy of a stop?" We had been told nothing so far.

In his understandable English with a strong Spanish accent, he replied, "Well, this is a cave that was found several decades ago by an Englishman. He discovered a strange old skin of some unknown animal and sent it on to England. So now we're going to see an empty cave."

He said this so laconically, with such a deadpan expression, I laughed my way through the 400-foot long cave. In fact, there was a statue of what the animal might have looked like. It was similar to a mylodon, a giant ground sloth larger than a bear, alive perhaps 10,000 years ago. In spite of his less than enthusiastic description and build-up, I discovered that this very cave was one of his most favorite stopping places along the 25-day route. I never was to know why.

The rather short, 5½ foot, classic Spanish-looking Manuel had the requisite moustache and wore glasses. Unprepossessing at first, his impressive accomplishments in the climbing world became apparent only slowly and through much inquisitiveness on my part. He had been one of the first to introduce modern climbing techniques to Chile, after attending climbing schools in Chamonix, France. He had used his knowledge in a practical way when he worked in the mines of northern Chile. Some of the mining activity there occurs at more than 15,000 feet. He was never really clear as to his actual duties, but I gathered that he explored many of the peaks in that area. Not famous for first ascents, he had gained a reputation for guiding thousands of travelers throughout the Chilean Andes.

This was a quiet man who assessed things carefully and perceptively. He could admire Mabel for her courage in taking her 200+ pounds to a far-off country. He took time to draw out Sharon from her shell so that she could allow herself to enjoy the trip. Sensitive but self-contained, Manuel spoke well for Chile.

The other Chilanos who became involved with our group at various times were also wholly enjoyable. Jorgé could melt any woman's heart with his smile, yet never abused that ability. He guided us through the Lake District and was sincere in his enjoyment at sharing his country with tourists. Even our bus driver for this area, Harrison, added his personality to the traveling. He became very forthcoming on a boat trip on Lake Llanquihue.

He disarmingly asked me if I was married, but only as a point of reference. He was unused to seeing fortyish women who weren't married traveling alone. He proceeded to describe the value Chilanos put on faithfulness in marriage. Yet many easy-going Chilanos often stray while married and are not chastised for it. Apparently, unfaithfulness was accepted but not valued. The casual manner of these people was, to them, favored.

Harrison went on to describe his experiences in the military when Salvador Allende was in power. Allende is recognized as the first Marxist to be elected in South America. His nationalization and collectivization was not accepted by most, and Allende was deposed in a coup d'etat in 1973 and replaced by Augusto Pinochet who ruled by a military junta for the next 17 years.

In Allende's time, every male was required to serve two years in the military with allowances given students to serve in the summers. When asked how he felt serving under Allende, Harrison was somewhat disingenuous. He prefaced his comments by insisting he was apolitical. He explained that during the latest election, he was quite sick. The police came to his door inquiring as to why he hadn't voted. His doctor's written diagnosis was the only thing that could officially excuse him.

Duly noting that differences existed between the election processes of the United States and Chile, he proceeded as I listened intently. He indicated that, while in the army, he was made to do many activities he found personally reprehensible. Trying to break through the Spanish accent barrier, I heard him talk of torture, which included even the classic pulling of fingernails.

In response to "Why?" he replied that he was ordered to do these things, and what else could he do? He said it so clearly and practically, I didn't react. I found myself sympathizing with what then was a young man trying to survive under unusual circumstances. I was glad Allende was no longer in power and that Harrison had found a wife and contentment in a new life. Most Chilanos seemed to similarly manage.

Harrison became the first real admirer of my bagpipe playing in Chile. After flying from Santiago to Puerto Montt, a town of about 100,000 in 1988, but looking about half that size, our entourage boarded a small tour bus and headed back north to visit the Lake District. We were now officially beginning our tour of Patagonia, though we really hadn't reached what some would consider Patagonia yet.

Our first stop for lunch was at a restaurant adjoining a lovely beach. The sun bounced happily off the water and drew me away from eating and to the almost deserted beach. A slight breeze cooled the air to a pleasant bagpipe playing temperature. I let the others indulge in feeding their faces; I would feed my soul with the music of the gods. Across the water in the far distance, this time not occluded by

A Uruguayan who was camping in the nearby greenbelt emerged from his tent in total bemusement. He had heard pipes before in some long-forgotten circumstance.

haze, were more snow-capped mountains. I felt a strong call to play, and out came the pipes. Surely no police would interrupt my communion with this pure environment.

I walked down the stony beach a ways to distance myself from the restaurant where many of the others had become ensconced. Sound carries near water, however, and I was still unsure about my group's reaction to some weird bagpipe player in their midst. Two others from the group had joined me out of curiosity. Again, I pressed Cathy and Jim, the architect, to act as photographers. Why not have a record of this bizarre marriage of bagpipes and Patagonia? I played, posed, and otherwise thoroughly enjoyed myself.

Harrison came charging from the bus on a dead run. I thought for sure the restaurant owners had objected, and he was going to ask me to stop. Instead, he displayed wild enthusiasm—I cannot call it anything else—for my bagpipes. In short sentences, out of breath from sprinting and perhaps from the excitement, he explained that he had never heard any sound like it before. And he loved it!

Moreover, the restaurant owners had expressed delight at the unexpected entertainment and felt lucky to have this added attraction near their business. When would I learn that bagpipes generally really appeal to most people? When would I lose my over-sensitivity for others when playing?

For the next few days that Harrison was with us, he was the most attentive audience I was to ever have. Manuel quietly indicated he was going to cry from nostalgia. I was at a loss to figure out what he was talking about. He had, in fact, lived in England for seven years and had grown accustomed to the sound of the pipes there. As some of my group finished lunch, they, too, were drawn to the sound. Little did they know my pipes would be an ever-present commodity on their journey. I was relieved to find an initial receptiveness from my fellow travelers.

As we discussed Manuel's and Harrison's histories respective to their experiences with and without the bagpipes, I was in the process of changing my film. It was before the days of digital cameras. My Olympus OM-B had never really impressed me. After the minor headaches it gave me in China and Japan, I had bought a back-up small point-and-shoot 35mm camera, just in case. Any photos of note, though, would come from my Olympus.

As I began to rewind my first roll, I detected a strange ease to the rewind button. As I cranked away, a troublesome doubt grew with great reluctance. Something was wrong. My eyes closed in slow realization and disbelief. How could I have committed the classic mistake of an amateur by forgetting to put film in the camera? The photos in the Plaza des Armes of Santiago would be only in my memory! There was nothing to do but put a roll in the camera and be glad the camera wasn't broken. The camera owner's head—mine!—was the only thing broken, if just temporarily.

I drew only a sparse few others from hiding. A Uruguayan who was camping in the nearby greenbelt emerged from his tent in total bemusement. He had heard pipes before in some long-forgotten circumstance. In passable English, he expressed curiosity as to the whys and wherefores of the pipes and my playing. I was to hear these same queries over and over for the next few weeks. I'm not sure I was ever able to adequately answer some of these questions, for them or for myself.

Why had I brought them to Chile? For practice? To break the ice with the locals? To see if music really is the international language? A latent exhibitionism? All of the above perhaps? Some questions delved into the actual techniques. What did the drones do and how was the sound maintained? These I could answer to some satisfaction. The others were left hanging.

Why do you want to see our country? Do you like it? Are you enjoying yourself? What do you think of our country? These were the questions from the locals to us about their country. The Chilanos were very concerned with our impression of Chile. They wanted very much for us to like their country and the inhabitants. I found it easy to answer in the affirmative.

Some children gathered on the beach. I was to find that children were the most open and unabashed bagpipe appreciators anywhere. Children seem to have a special fondness for the sound and invariably display eyes as big as bright moons. These particular children spoke no English but quietly sat down next to me and listened politely and clapped when I finished. I figured that sign language was needed to complete the cycle. I held my hands to my ears and they laughed. Some barrier had been broken, and I felt totally comfortable in Chile from that day on.

We continued driving north to the Lake District, and I was adjusting to group travel again somewhat reluctantly. We stopped at a particularly interesting seafood market. In contrast to the people in Santiago, these Chilanos exhibited more Indian elements in their facial features—darker skin, narrowed eyes, sharper features and less European. This influence would increase as we headed south. I saw and felt no evidence of racial problems, though I'm told they exist. The settlers had their own way of solving most of the racial problems that have caused so many difficulties in other countries where settlers have met natives. Here, they apparently either killed them or married them!

I was computing this information and enjoying the steamy smells of all the fish when I realized that the bus pulling away in the distance was mine! I pondered the situation without panic and hoped the bus was only moving ahead a short distance to repark. As it kept increasing the distance and speed, I realized I might have more time in this market than I had anticipated. I wondered how long it might be before they discovered I was missing.

I kept walking, reserving judgment until the bus was all but out of sight. At about that moment, it stopped. Manuel jumped out at a dead run back to the market. When he saw me, he pulled up with a smile claiming it had all been a joke. I knew better and would not let him squirm out of his dereliction of duty. He had forgotten me, and I would give him a hard time about it, all the while laughing inside.

Not being able to stop at will along the road was frustrating, and I was anxious to jog at our stops when I could, to make up for the lack of physical activity and for spending so much time in the bus. I made note that, in Santiago, I saw only one woman jogging in shorts: women wore sweat pants rolled up or other attire longer than shorts. While it was 90°F. in Santiago, and shorts would have been nice, the accepted attire was more restrained. The rest of Chile imposed no such problems because a cool 40-60° F. made running pants just fine.

We were now in the Lake District gazing at the beautiful, perfectly conical-shaped Fuji-like volcano, Mt. Osorno, rising above Lake Todos los Santos. Separate volcanoes ringed the area, conjuring up memories of my days in

the Pacific Northwest again. We arrived at our hotel in
Fruitillar at dusk as the sun was setting across the lake,
casting an afterglow of pinkish shades on all the peaks.

I was starting to feel like I was getting close to the
Patagonia I had pictured, though, in reality, I was still well
north of what is considered Patagonia. We were certainly
close to mountains, but we were yet to reach the rugged
barrenness of the South. This was still a resort area; people
were trying to sun bathe on the beach. Why women could
wear revealing bikinis but not jog in shorts was a paradox.

In the tourist mode, our group joined the crowd taking
the lake cruise on Lake Llanguihue. The boat was built for
Patagonian weather and most of the seating was inside.
However, the day was gorgeous, if cool, and the travelers
with intrepid spirits crowded onto the open fantail. Low-
lying fog was lingering hither and yon, obscuring portions
of the peaks, but revealing enough to draw our eyes to the
emerging summits.

I started to get the familiar rumblings of inspiration
for music. As it happened, one of our couple's
anniversary was that day. Cajoled by others, I allowed
my arm to be twisted and brought out the pipes
once again.

With some advance preparation and prompting, I
played "Happy Birthday" while our group sang "Happy

Anniversary" to the lucky couple. I had made friends for life with this small act and furthered the cause of personal relationships and more pipe playing later in the trip.

The other 50 or so passengers were bemused by the scene and sound, and the cameras I was finally getting used to were flashing away at will. But the sound of the boat's motor was more than a match for the pipes, and my enthusiasm dwindled rapidly. I chose to stuff them away in exchange for talking to a very friendly, good-looking Australian. Pipes to him were no big thing, but he had hardly expected them in Patagonia.

We chugged along 20 miles of shoreline, peering at steep mountains and vast forests, each bend in the lake providing more impressive views than the last. Waterfalls peeked out everywhere, indicating the massive snows up above. We passed islands and stopped offshore to load and unload passengers and/or mail.

As we reached the end of the lake and docked, the clouds had totally dissipated, and we were in full sun. I quickly ate lunch at the tourist-loving restaurant, hiked to the nearby falls, which had more people clambering around its flanks than its appearance deserved. I made my way to an open picnic area down the path.

Out of sight of the restaurant did not mean out of earshot, as I had learned several days before. In less than a minute the familiar crowd gathered. After a few short tunes, our time was up; the boat was scheduled to head back. As we packed up, a fellow from England sidled over to me to say that that was the greatest sound he'd heard since he'd been in Chile!

Mt. Osorno, a fairly active, now glaciated volcano, was out in full splendor. A ski area exists on its flanks, and like so many other mountains, it looks deceptively easy to climb. Weather and snow conditions, however, can make this a killer mountain, and many have died attempting its 8,727-foot summit. As in so many cases, most of these deaths could have been prevented by common sense and turning back before a situation worsened. The mountain somehow gets blamed in these incidents. Yet, the mountains survive; the people do not.

We had passed inhabited cabins on the shore only rarely on our boat trip. These places could be reached only by boat, I presumed; their inhabitants must live a precarious but quiet existence. The view of these mountains, no doubt, provided much sustenance for them.

17

FARTHER SOUTH AND CHILOE

I could see what was coming and obliged by playing "Scotland the Brave." We played a few notes together, and, to our mutual disappointment, realized our instruments were not in the same key. There was no compatibility between instruments, but the musicians could appreciate each other's music and abilities. The international language of music had emerged but not as successfully as we would have liked.

Surprising us on our drive was the curious, culturally distinct island of Chiloe. Chiloe is a large island off the west coast of Chile, roughly 50 miles by 130 miles in size. The inhabitants here maintain a separate identity from the other Chilanos. I sensed a special charm to the island.

The ferry had taken only a half hour from the mainland, but this low, flat, non-descript offset island lent an air of singularity from the Patagonia known to most visitors. The 100-inch-a-year rainfall provides ever-present mists lending credence to the local belief that Chiloe is an island of disembodied spirits.

We were in luck. Festival time had arrived in Castro, the picturesque town founded in the 1560s by the Spanish, lying on the inside coast from the sea. We were entertained the night we arrived with a folk music festival of pure Chiloan music. This was music particular to Chiloe Island, not found anywhere else in Chile, according to the locals. If I had been in doubt as to the strong German influence in Chile, I became convinced this night. The music groups that were to demonstrate their skills would usually include the requisite guitar or two, some kind of drum, and an accordion.

The addition of the accordion certainly made the sleepy and otherwise disinterested listener at least stand up and take notice. The accordion, though played all over the world today, screamed its German roots. The drums in Chiloe were played with one soft stick and a hard one on the rim. Three-quarter time was the accepted tempo, with few others in evidence.

The first few songs were of interest and mildly entertaining. However, the same constant beat on the same instruments, accompanied by questionable singing abilities, quickly convinced visitors to turn their attention elsewhere. Even though the music employed vibrant rhythm, modern influences were making themselves known, for better or for worse.

I observed the audience and noticed something strange. First and foremost, was the absence of any drunken behavior. In fact, very few of the several hundred in attendance were drinking alcohol at all, in spite of its availability. Most were quite content to sip away on soda. I asked an English-speaking Chiloto teacher why this was the case. She replied, "I don't know. A lot of drinking just isn't a big part of our culture."

Maybe as a consequence of this and other cultural factors, the crowd was an attentive audience, and a very polite one at that. They loved what they heard, were proud of it, and showed their appreciation in spite of the less than stellar quality. I've observed many audiences during many a school program in a small town where I taught. Standard procedure was for anyone to get up and

walk around at any given time, or even in the middle of
a performance. Here I was, under a tent in a "backwater"
nowhere, and yet people displayed exceptional manners.

While I was distracted, Manuel quietly suggested to
the organizers of the event that I play my bagpipes to
this audience. While tempted in some ways to join the
festivities, I had completely understood that it was clear
this was a totally Chilote performance, celebrating their
music. Before I could voice my reservations, Manuel
was talking to the emcee about squeezing me onto the
program during one of the breaks. I was hesitant but
didn't flatly refuse, either.

The situation took care of itself with a little help from
me. I enjoyed as much of the evening's entertainment as
I could and decided an orderly retreat was the better part
of valor. Later, Manuel told me that the concert organizers
looked for me shortly after I left during the first break.
I felt I had showed respect for the local culture by not
interrupting the music flow with something other than
Chilote music. It may have been a missed opportunity,
but I was happy with my decision.

In fact, later that evening, I was to hear music more
to my liking, and, in some ways, more identifiable to the
Andes. On my return to the hotel, I passed the central
plaza where activity abounded at night. I heard faint

strains of street music on the far side of the plaza where a small crowd had gathered. A traveling quartet had riveted the nightwalkers with music of a more Andean flavor. They played, variously, flute, guitar, mandolin, a lute-like instrument, and drums.

I considered jamming with them but thought better of it when they passed the hat. I feared they would see me as an interloper, cutting into their share of the profits. Besides, a bagpipe would have no trouble completely drowning out mandolins and guitars, as well as not being able to be in tune with them. Fun thought, though.

We left Harrison and Chiloe, and, after an eight-hour boat ride, arrived in Patagonia proper, in a small town called Chaiten. The conveyance ferrying us across Golfo de Ancud was strictly utilitarian. But I was relieved not to be involved in another tourist operation. Here was a scow designed to carry goods and a few locals from island to island.

However, the seaworthiness of this steamer was dubious. Passengers outnumbered the cramped seats, and I spent most of my time braving the cold elements out on deck. Whiling the hours away practicing the pipes would have been a good idea. Unfortunately, the only area available would have squeezed me between some exhaust pipe and part of a boiler. I decided to devote my time to chanter practice and retain my anonymity as just another passenger.

I was aroused from my practicing when I heard some beautiful sonorous sounds from around the corner of the bulwark. As I approached, a small group was clustering around a little Spanish-looking fellow in a ratty old poncho. I recognized the instrument he was playing as a *quena*, a bamboo flute played like a recorder. I listed to the Andean-flavored tunes and wondered if a Scottish chanter would blend with a South American *quena*. Manuel helped interpret.

"What is your instrument called?" he asked with sincere interest.

Once again, I explained with patience and respect due a fellow musician, "This is a chanter. I learned my fingering techniques on this before I learned to play the bagpipes."

He had a faint idea of what bagpipes were when I used the word *gaita*. *Gaita* is the Spanish version of bagpipes. "What key is your instrument?"

I could see what was coming and obliged by playing "Scotland the Brave." We played a few notes together, and, to our mutual disappointment, realized our instruments were not in the same key. There was no compatibility between instruments, but the musicians could appreciate each other's music and abilities. The international language of music had emerged but not as successfully as we would have liked.

The *gaita* comes from Spain and differs from the Scottish Highland bagpipe in several ways. The *gaita* has a bass drone and may have one or two additional drones playing the tonic and dominant notes. The two extra drones will stick out from the right arm of the player instead of being placed next to the base drone as in the Scottish bagpipes. Extra pressure on the bag can cause a second octave unlike the Scottish bagpipe. Other differences exist causing different sounds. But then there are dozens of variants for bagpipes around the world. According to Wikipedia, the *gaita* was popular in the Middle Ages, then declined in popularity but has regained acceptance in the last few decades.

Chaiten was a small, dusty, uninspiring town, which we left early the next morning. The announcement of the completion of the Pan-American Highway seems to have been nothing more than a good publicity stunt at the time. The promoters had ignored the fact that a few bridges were still needed. Fortunately, there were short "ferry" rides on rafts, which carried two or three vehicles. They were pulled across the rivers by some form of come-along. Time spent waiting for our turn to cross provided a good opportunity to entertain the troops with my bagpipes.

Pablo, our official lead guide, had finally joined us in Chaiten and was eager to hear them. He insisted that I was the very first piper to play in the area. Once again, spirits seems to revive with the sound of the pipes. Everyone returned to the bus on the other side of the river with freshened outlooks and eager anticipation to see what was around the next bend.

We arrived in a fishing resort motel away from any town for the night. The quiet restfulness was a relief from battling the bouncing bus. Little did we know that the bouncing bus would become a true nemesis in the coming days. As of now, it was a relatively comfortable means of transportation.

The small nearby lake provided reflections of the green birch forest. And strains of Mozart could be heard from the cassette tape recorder in the restaurant. Our neat little homemade cabins came complete with wood stoves, which were put to good use this night.

As "tourista" attacked me the next morning, I was wishing for more than one bathroom for the six of us. It took me twenty minutes to clean out my insides and lose several pounds in the process. Fortunately, the others weren't similarly affected at the time. Their turns would come later.

18
FINALLY! PATAGONIA!

Everyone, apparently, was hiding in his or her houses.
Again, it was the children who fearlessly approached this
wonderfully weird noise. As more and more cherubs magically
appeared, I marched around the block, playing and collecting
the children as I went. I truly felt like the pied piper.

The next day would be a highlight of my travels throughout the world. By the next mid-morning, we were passing through a town called Puyuhuapi. The names of Chilean towns were a strange blend of Spanish and Indian, and this time I expected to see strong Indian features in the residents. When we arrived, I saw no people whatsoever. This was reminiscent of a scene from "High Noon" when the town was empty of residents and dust swirled everywhere. We usually drew curious onlookers, polite and friendly, but none appeared in this town. As we stopped to check in with the police of the region, our bus-weary travelers slowly disembarked to have a look around.

The warm sun and clear sky invited music. As I struck in the first few notes, small, round, definitely Indian faces appeared at the windows for a quick moment before emptying out into the streets at my feet. Everyone, apparently, was hiding in his or her houses. Again, it was the children who fearlessly approached this wonderfully weird noise. When more and more cherubs magically appeared, I marched around the block, playing and collecting the children as I went. I truly felt like the pied piper.

The fascination emanating from their eyes was humbling. One little girl with red overalls and unblinking eyes looked like she was watching a new god. I think that if I had swept her up onto the bus to take her home with me, she would have been delighted. And I have to admit I was uncharacteristically tempted.

The children enjoyed the pied piper of Patagonia.

As a teacher, I enjoyed my students, but I've never been a mom. The kid gene had missed me. Strange that this particular incident would create those maternal instincts.

The only adult I saw in my marching around the town was a toothless, plump old gal carrying a fish in one hand and a tattered basket in the other. I happened to come to the end of a tune as she passed. She had started to speak before I had stopped playing. In a mouthful of rapid-fire Spanish, perhaps with some native Indian language thrown in, she addressed my playing and me. Even if I hadn't caught *muy bonita,* which means very beautiful, I think I could have understood her meaning. Her kind eyes and tone of voice clearly indicated admiration.

Manuel was there again to help with translation and added that she thought the sounds were some of the most beautiful she'd ever heard. She had only slowed her walk as she paid me these compliments then continued her mission without breaking stride. Although I must have been a break in her monotonous duties, she would not be deterred in her daily operation. Still, her openness, complete wonderment and respect for my playing thoroughly warmed me.

As I packed up to leave, the children had grown braver and clustered around me. I hurriedly swung my camera around to snap a quick shot. Swiftness wasn't necessary as all the smiling faces clambered to be included in the photo. I felt they had all become my friends in the short fifteen minutes of "touring" their village. I would never see these children again, but I hoped I showed them that being different was okay. I hoped I had brought some joy into their lives that day. They certainly had into mine.

We were now approaching the Patagonia I had always imagined. Driving along fjords surrounded by glaciated mountain peaks was more like it. The road took on horrific curves that never stopped. We climbed over a mountain that required so many switchbacks, the squiggles ran off their warning signs! The bus unhappily ground up the steepness while we leisurely gazed across the valleys.

There was an element of rain forest here. The barrenness would come later. After all day imagining myself with a machete hacking my way through this untouched terrain, we reached Puerto Cisnes, a small village relying on the sea for communication. We had passed only three cars that day, and even the most intrepid traveler might want to avoid this backwater, if possible—or actively seek it out, depending on the traveler.

However, this town was definitely to my liking—small, colorful, and lively. People were bustling everywhere doing all sorts of odd jobs. The beach was adorned with fishing dories dragged up and tied to some makeshift land anchors, waiting for the tide to come in and to be put to use again. Men were patching and scraping away at real and imaginary ills on their boats, others were off-loading large pieces of driftwood for either firewood or for some other unknown use.

There was even a "circus" in town. As far as I could see, this consisted of a few llamas or guanacos tied to a fence for everyone to pet. My temptation to again join the festivities that night faded as my exhaustion increased. The next morning, I learned that what I had missed was nothing more than a teen dance. Still, I hadn't experienced such a thing in Chile and would have liked to. Maybe I would have had better luck than I did with the dance in China.

The Chilanos have some interesting ideas that may bemuse travelers. At dinner that night, I noticed a plastic bag filled with water hanging from the ceiling. The use of this befuddled us all. Nothing would do but for us to ask outright. We were told that this was Chilean mosquito and fly repellant! I cannot attest to its effectiveness nor how it was supposed to work; it was too cold that time of year to worry about mosquitoes or flies anyway.

Meanwhile we were trying to concentrate on eating our non-descript unknown beef/pork/lamb dinner. My mouth was watering for some wonderful fresh fish off of a local boat. We were reduced to the "group" fare, which I had avoided earlier in the trip. As a result, earlier in the trip I had enjoyed the best salmon I'd ever had. But tonight I put on a brave front with some kind of tasteless, bland meat.

I have never been a fan of flan, a custard dessert with soft caramel topping, nor would I be after three straight weeks of being served flan for every single dessert in Chile. Whether the Chilanos felt it was a native dish the tourists expected, or whether they just always have it, flan was the dessert of the day—every day! In addition, all their fresh fruit was imported. We were to have canned peaches and pears whenever we were served fruit.

Coihaique was a town of fewer than 50,000 nestled in the mountains as well as being Pablo's home. There really wasn't much to see in the town itself, and I wondered if we were there because Pablo could spend two nights with his new young wife or whether it was on our route anyway. Our special treat was a dinner in a restaurant he had some financial interest in.

We were the only dinner guests there and were treated with total deference. Hors d'ouerves were offered on silver platters as we sipped pisco sours. I was starting to really feel relaxed and enjoy myself.

Entertainment was forthcoming with dancers and singers. The *huaso* dancers and folk singers are traditional entertainment in Chile. The males are bedecked with leather chaps, small ponchos, wide, flat–brimmed hats and those great sexy, fist-sized spurs we had seen on the road several days before. The males dance around colorfully attired women, waving handkerchiefs in the air as a flirtation device. The singing is accompanied with guitar and accordion with a Spanish flavor. This is the dance shown to all tourists and was seemingly a source of pride to the Chilanos. Fortunately, we found the dancing and singing very enjoyable since we would see it many more times.

I was completely relaxed, enjoying the entertainment and pisco sours—Chilean pisco and Pica lime—when Pablo approached me with that eager look of his. I discerned what he wanted, and I tried to retreat into a corner. This was no time to play bagpipes. I wanted to hear local fare, not my own stuff. But Pablo was insistent, and I perceived a potential loss of face on his part if I didn't play.

The dancers and singers had stepped back for a break, and I entered the void. I was feeling awkward once again at subjecting my group to more pipes. But when I looked at the faces of the Chilanos—dancers, singers, waiters, and Pablo—I experienced a now familiar sensation. Here again were fellow musicians who were hearing new music. They obviously were enjoying what they were hearing. Their surprised looks were so overwhelming, I couldn't help but chuckle to myself. It is nigh impossible to play pipes while laughing but I carried on, nonetheless.

The disparity in music styles was striking; I think we all were a bit awe-struck by the bizarre but pleasing contrast. I was glad to have been a bit loose from the pisco sours; they do wonders for stage fright, which you'd think I would be well over by now.

I had played earlier in the afternoon in the central plaza. An appreciative crowd had gathered at a respectful distance, and I played without my usual self-consciousness. I wanted some more photographs of the mixture of cultures and gave my camera to Manuel who was becoming a jack-of-all-trades. I played as he took photos and then tried to rewind the film.

He had retired behind a tree, but I sensed something was wrong again. The police station was across the street, and a policeman was slowly approaching with uncertainty in his eyes. But it was not the policeman that I had in my sights; I noticed Manuel with a strange look on his face. Before I stopped playing and approached Manuel, I knew I had more camera problems. He had broken the film while rewinding it and opened the camera exposing the film! Oh, for digital cameras and iPhones of today!

I was pretty resigned at this moment to throwing the thing away. Dejectedly stashing it and the pipes in my daypack, I let Manuel treat me to a beer. Applause from a group of teenage boys as I left the plaza helped my spirits only a little. At least I had left before the policeman reached me. But, yet again, I was left without any photos of the experience.

Heading south without a working camera, I was getting close to the Patagonian ice caps. The day we spied the northern ice cap produced a feeling of finally having arrived. Pablo was leading us into the unknown.

We had two bridges of dubious quality to cross, one of which had just been completed as a temporary bridge. But that bridge would come the next day. Today we would catch glimpses of the ice cap from a lake steamer, which took us across Lago Carrera to Puerto Sanchez. The boat provided a unique and picturesque opportunity for pipe

Chilean trawler provided scenic setting for playing.

playing. The one family on board seemed to enjoy the odd entertainment.

There were no roads to the tiny village of Puerto Sanchez. There was a rather large mine of tin, magnesium and zinc, which kept the town of 150 people employed. Incredibly, these minerals were being shipped to Belgium for processing. Ah, the wonders of a small world!

The owner of the mine also ran the motel and was as warm, friendly, and patient with our questions as he could be. I was curious as to what he thought of these strange Americans visiting his town. When we disembarked from the boat, I had looked back at our group. A more touristy group would be hard to find. The most conspicuous trait was the ridiculous hats everyone wore. They varied from the redneck baseball caps to sailor's hats to floppy-brimmed old ladies' hats. If I had debated wearing any kind of hat up to that point, I no longer gave it a further thought. We came in all sizes with all the requisite cameras hanging from every appendage. No wonder Americans have a varied reputation abroad.

We were similarly attired for a boat ride the next day. We had spent the night in an out-of-the-way cabin with no other guests. We soon learned why we were shepherded so far away from anything when we saw

Pablo returning from his morning's all-important fishing expedition. This was one of Pablo's favorite fishing spots!

The same lake trawler ferried us down toward the sea to curious carbonate formations. Of more interest to me was one of the deck hands. This fellow was full of happiness, which he constantly displayed with a five-tooth smile stretching across his face. He obviously found us entertaining, if not a bit bizarre. He became our rower on the trawler's leaky rowboat; we rode four at a time around the formations. For some reason, the rower and the rowboat were a perfect blend and contributed to my extreme pleasure that morning.

We were apparently some of the few Americans who managed to reach these towns. And we were to be the very first to travel over the next section of road. Returned to the highway by our friends in the trawler, we got on the bus, now our home, and took off.

We were about to experience the other bridge, which had recently been built to enable travel on this new section of road. A

The bus had a mere one inch to spare on either side.

modern concrete bridge structure was in the making, but not completed. The sight of the temporary one had us scrambling out of the bus without any hesitation. The overwhelming consensus was to walk across the bridge before the bus driver negotiated the rickety, makeshift crossing. Once he was safely across, we assumed we had done the hard part.

Down the road a short distance, Pablo informed us there was one more obstacle. Another old bridge was slung across a ferry-less river. Only this one was rated for a few tons less than we were. We were happy not to be the driver, who made a point of telling us he couldn't swim. We evacuated the bus again and hurriedly walked ahead so that we'd be on the other side before the driver started across.

Not only was the bridge structurally weak, the bus had a mere one inch to spare on either side. A closer fit couldn't be had. Proceeding slowly and with all of us holding our collective breaths, the bus crept the 50 yards and finally joined us on the other side of the river as we cheered the prowess of the driver.

Farther up the river another modern concrete bridge was being built for future use. We chose this spot to have lunch and enjoy the loosened tensions. I entertained the nearby bridge workers with some pipe playing, and we continued on our way, knowing that no other group would experience such excitement.

19
ARGENTINA'S CONTRASTS

On the final approach, Mt. Fitzroy was hidden due to the steepness of the moraine we were climbing. It had been teasing us all morning, hiding behind some freshly arrived clouds. Rounding the bend I gasped at the full glory of Mt. Fitzroy in a pure azure day, devoid of any clouds.

The Argentine pampas sound more romantic than they are in reality—by a lot. The first two hours of driving through them was sufficient to give a traveler all they'd ever want to know about the pampas. Unfortunately, we were to experience one more day than planned on the already endless pampas, due to some sort of bureaucratic bungling. The extra 75 miles we had to drive north did not add to the "Patagonia experience" in any positive way.

We left the glaciated peaks and valleys of Chile to cross Paso Roballos onto the Argentine plains. Miles and miles and miles of sage and fine dust drifting into the bus through loose-fitting windows did nothing for our psyches or throats.

Pampas to me had meant "grasslands." My high school textbook said so. I kept looking for the endless tall grass. All I felt was grit. My contact lenses stayed in only because I'm stubborn and vain. There is a dry western part of the pampas, mostly barren and a humid east. I, obviously, was experiencing the dry West, which lacked the romance the word "pampas" had initially instilled in me.

Behind us in Chile, we had crossed one valley, which had presented us with an interesting proposition. As we approached a broad open pass, the road had become less and less distinct. We had left the Pan American Highway proper and headed east. After we laboriously and slowly wended our way up wide S-curves, our road became more of a cow and sheep path. We paralleled a glacier-melt stream for some time until it was obvious we would have to cross. No ferries or bridges here.

Given the temperature of the day and season, the crossing could be easy or impossible. On a hot day, by afternoon, the stream would have swollen with melt water into a raging torrent. In cold months, a trickle would be all that was found. This day was somewhere in between.

The bus coasted to a stop, and Manuel and Pablo eagerly jumped out in boyish anticipation. The stream looked deep and fast flowing. Without so much as a moment's hesitation, Pablo plowed into the water gesturing for Manuel not to bother taking off his shoes and to join him. Arm-in-arm they charged through the freezing water up to their thighs, looking for the shallowest passageway for the bus.

Once on the other side, they motioned for the bus driver to proceed. Shaking our heads in disbelief, convinced that we had no chance whatsoever of succeeding, we hung our heads out the window to anticipate where we would get stuck. Our bus moved carefully and deliberately through the swift-flowing water. Three-quarters of the way through, we slowed, on the verge of a stall, but amazingly the bus kept chugging away. And then we were on the other side! We unloaded to marvel at the accomplishment and to again compliment the driver.

"It's a good thing we have a four-wheel drive bus for these things," I remarked in relief.

"Who told you it was a four-wheel drive?" Manuel replied in a voice filled with as much relief as my own.

I was glad not to have known that ours was a regular mortal bus. Had the bus gotten bogged down, it might still be there. There were many, many miles on either side of us with no habitation at all. I have no idea whether there were any contingency plans. I feel fairly certain there were none. On looking back, I wished that we had encountered some form of difficulty, if only to add to the uniqueness of the experience. However, if it had meant more days on the pampas, I would retract any such desire.

More pampas, more sage-like vegetation, more dust, a few guanacos and rheas, maybe an armadillo or two, and more dust. Spirits were sagging and so were our bodies. One look around the bus revealed ten people drooping against the windows with eyes shut against the grit and minds dealing with the situation. I even joined Cathy in looking for birds. Unable to sleep or read, I gazed at the brown nothingness and tried not to think about my developing cough. We were all pampas-weary and gauzy-eyed when we reached "the canyon."

The canyon would be one of the more remarkable sights in all of Patagonia. In contrast to the lazy rolling endless pampas, this canyon appeared as a geologic anomaly. Pinturas River Canyon contains the Cueva de las Manos or Cave of the Hands. These caves are painted with stenciled hands, pictures of animals, and hunting scenes. The paintings date to between 7,000 and 11,000 years ago. Because we were so far out in the middle of nowhere, I found it incredible to see a visitor's cabin at the trailhead. Somehow, in the course of man's wanderings, someone had discovered these very ancient cliff paintings and deemed them worthy of an official hut.

This meant that, in the course of mankind's history, one or more persons had made these paintings in their wanderings of the interminably endless pampas. The paintings were mostly of hands that looked like someone had mouth-sprayed paint around them on the rocks. Why man was there in the first place 7,000 years ago was mystery enough. Why we were there was another mystery. I wondered how out of the way this was to our regular route.

Skeptical as to the authenticity of the hands, I was taken with the magical etherealness of the geology of the place. The trail sidestepped along the cliffs, as paintings led to more paintings. I continued walking while others dropped out. Vaguely aware that I couldn't go too far lest the bus leave without me again, I stopped at a point where the canyon began to widen. A half-hearted effort at a yodel produced an incredible echo that begged for more. But somehow the sound was not in keeping with the eerie quiet, and I stopped to return to the group.

As I rejoined the others, a silent shadow overhead darkened our path. What better place to sight our first condor! It was soaring on the thermals and, no doubt, checking us out. We were disturbing its home territory and we didn't belong. After the mad rush at photographic efforts, we retired to the visitor's cabin for lunch. I felt like I should make an offering to such a magical place and dared to take out my pipes.

With visions of great photos of my pipes and me in front of the canyon running in my head, I hastened to get ready. In the process, one of those drone reeds fell into the bag again.

Pablo was making moves to leave, so I quickened my actions only to have the reed actually break inside the bag. I could have played using the other drones if I could have corked up the reedless drone. But my corks and other reeds were back in the bus 100 yards away!

People were loading now and my opportunity to echo bagpipes across this magnificent place was fading. I deemed the incident a sign from the gods; I figured the message was that I should not play bagpipes in that other world. Disappointed, I gathered up the pieces and threw myself in the bus ready to spend a few hours on repairing my bagpipes. At least I would have something to while away the hours on the tortuous bus ride across more pampas.

The night was spent in some now nameless Argentinian town. Our next objective was Mt. Fitzroy, a famous and infamous rock peak in the annals of climbing. As we arrived the next day, my high expectations of a numbing sight were realized. Our efforts to reach this nirvana of mountain peaks had all been worthwhile.

We piled into the hostel in late afternoon, time enough to see the huge phallic peak poking its head through the clouds. I offered more bagpipe tunes to the weather gods, and this time they were accepted. We waited for tomorrow and our all-day hiking trip in what would be fine, clear weather.

My body was aching for exercise. It was not to be disappointed this day. We left the spartan hostel at a leisurely 9:30 a.m., with me eagerly urging the others to get going. We would not return until 7:30 p.m. Views of glacier-carved valleys were back with us, and lush forests filled with strange birds accompanied us to "base camp."

Mercifully, only half of the group chose to make the hike, and at that, we broke into smaller, more tolerable groups of like ability. After reaching what was loosely termed base camp after many hours of hiking along a broad, open valley, we clambered up the last hour to a breath-taking viewpoint at a glacial tarn. On the final approach, Mt. Fitzroy was hidden due to the steepness of the moraine we were climbing. It had been teasing us all morning, hiding behind some freshly arrived clouds. Rounding the bend I gasped at the full glory of Mt. Fitzroy in a pure azure day, devoid of any clouds.

I had been eager to reach our objective and pounded ahead with a fair pace. I noticed that one of our members was keeping pace with me with heavy breathing and a look that said, "No woman is going to beat me up any trail." Normally, I would chuckle at such male ego problems, back off, and enjoy a more leisurely pace. I never enjoyed this type of competition. But Tony had set himself up as an authority on everything in countless discussions, and I was unsettled and unhappy with his company.

So, this time I decided I would at least make him work for the lead. I had a hunch that his labored breathing and unsteady pace belied a poorer condition than he implied he had. Early on, he mumbled some excuses about a cold he had had right before he left on the trip. Conveniently ignoring that this was more than two weeks ago, he only spurred my displeasure at his macho behavior. I would not be denied and charged on.

In the end, there was only a small satisfaction when I reached our destination first. After all, I was at least 15 years younger. He wasn't in bad shape for his age; it had just been his attitude that bothered me. But this was no time to be distracted by such pettiness.

Some joy was to be had in being the first to crest the top and round the corner. Without the distraction of mindless chatter, I was left alone to be awestruck with the first incredible views. Mt. Fitzroy stands 11,066 feet above sea level and the summit was several thousand feet above me. The sharp granite spire and formidable, sheer faces are impressive, standing out from the surrounding peaks.

East meets West here, and the weather dumps on that spot. I had tried not to think of the possibilities of arriving at that special place and never seeing it because of blanketing clouds. Such worry is useless and energy wasting. Besides, it hadn't happened. There I was with not a cloud in the sky, and only what seemed to be 50 mph winds to encounter!

In overwhelming excitement, I stumbled to a large rock, which afforded protection from the wind. Of

course, I immediately started to take out my bagpipes.
At that moment, a fellow approached from the opposite
direction. In accented English, he offered to take a photo
of me with my camera. I nodded assent since it was
difficult to hear human speech over the wind.

Mt. Fitzroy offered a cold windy spot for pipes.

"Just wait until I get my bagpipes ready," I screamed.

"Your what?"

"I carried my bagpipes up here to play in one of the most stirring places in the whole world. I'd like the photo to have my bagpipes in it."

I looked like I was doing battle with an octopus as I tried to keep the drones from being blown off my shoulder. The wind was whipping so ferociously, I could barely stand unaided.

"Do you have the picture yet?" I played only a few tunes before the wind chilled my fingers. He assured me he had, indeed, taken the photo. And this time, not only was there film in the camera, there was no breakage.

"Where are you from?" came the time-honored question.

" Colorado, United States," I replied proudly. "And you?"

"I am from Israel. But I have been studying in the U.S—in Fort Collins—Colorado!"

It was the small-world syndrome again. Here I was in a place that took at least three days to reach from the U.S. and another day of hiking. Now, however, there is a nearby international airport! This was not a typically crowded tourist spot. But I was face-to-face with someone who lived less than 60 miles from me. We chatted some more, and I turned to play some more tunes.

Only four expeditions had succeeded in reaching the summit of Mt. Fitzroy that year. Or was it four people? Whatever the case, many a climber had died trying through the years. It was first climbed in 1952 by a team from France of Lionel Terray and Guido Magnone. Since then, many have tried its sheer cliffs and battled its infamous weather. Named after Robert Fitzroy who was captain of the HMS Beagle, the ship that carried

Charles Darwin, the mountain has a reputation of being "ultimate." I was content with viewing it from my present perch.

Reluctantly, I retreated down the bluff out of the wind back to the base camp area where we'd left some of our group. I kept glancing back to drink in every bit that I could. I regretted having to hike back with the big group after such an intimate experience with the incredible spire and spirit of Fitzroy.

Two others felt similarly and, without a word, we quickened our pace and increased the distance between "them and us." After a while, I was ready to slack off and relax. But Jim, the 40-year-old architect, was in the lead. He hadn't gone the last mile to the viewpoint and was feeling the need to stretch out. His energy was catching and three of us kept charging.

I started to remember that Lou, behind me, was not only 70+ years old, he had one blind eye. He had been literally on my heels for two hours. I offered to let him go ahead of me. He declined and stayed close enough for his breath to practically be on my shoulder. I felt like I should be going faster, but we'd been out seven or eight hours by now, and I was feeling the affects of little exercise for the last two weeks and the strenuous hike to this point.

"Lou, are you sure you don't want to go ahead of me? I really feel like I'm slowing you down."

"No, you're doing just fine. No problem."

"But, Lou, you've been two feet behind me for miles. I'm sure I'm getting in your way," I said in desperation.

Then the truth came out. "Actually, I need to have some feet right in front of me to help with my depth perception. With my blind eye, I have trouble placing my feet."

So, I found out I was a seeing-eye dog of sorts. I enjoyed his company, though we said little, or maybe it was because we said little. We were filling ourselves with the brisk air and ever-surprising views and washing ourselves of pampas dust at the same time. I came to admire Lou very much. Not only was he in good shape but also his attitude was extremely positive.

We reached the trailhead to find the bus waiting to take us to a much sought-after beer. After a minute's rest, we realized the others would be another half hour or so behind us. We wondered why we should wait when beer was calling. Anyway, we were on a roll, and what was another two miles of flat walking to the hostel? Off we went on foot, with perhaps some idea of hitting the shower first. On that we were to be denied.

We reached the hostel shortly before the bus arrived with its load. We were all a bit late for dinner, and the hosts requested that we be seated right away. I had snuck upstairs to test the water, and sure enough, the hot water didn't come on until 8 p.m. anyway. When I finally got to the shower after waiting for several others who had raced up following dinner, the water was only lukewarm and a trickle at best. But I had enjoyed my beer.

Our hostel was the type of accommodation I enjoyed, beautifully situated but very modest. In fact, eight of the women in my group were plunked down in the same dorm room, complete with bunk beds. Ironically, I, the youngest of all but one by about 20 years, was the only one who had difficulty negotiating the climb up to the top bunk. My excuse was legitimate though: I had savored my share of a bottle of Glenlivet that evening with the men of the group while enjoying viewing the Southern Cross in the dark skies overhead.

I returned to the room with what seemed like a marvelous idea for some excitement and variety. Since the men were obviously too staid to concoct anything like a panty raid, I figured a jock raid would be just the thing to liven up the group. I wasn't completely surprised when I discerned total disinterest on the part of these 60+-year-old women. Still, I persisted and at

least managed to glean some interesting tidbits about
the sleeping habits of the husbands of these intrepid
travelers. These hearty souls had spirit, but not enough,
it turned out, to attempt a reverse panty raid.

Back to the pampas, we were on our way to Calafante,
a town heralded as a tourist center. At first glance,
I could discern no reason at all for the label. Later,
I did find a few tourist shops that afforded our first
opportunities to buy some local Argentinian goods.
In frustration, I could not find any of those marvelous
huge silver spurs the *huasos* used. Ads for various boat
rides and scenic tours finally convinced me that this
area was only the
gateway to scenic
attractions sought
by the Argentinians,
Chilanos, and a few
wayward Americans
and other travelers,

> There are few times in one's
> life when the visual sense is so
> impacted in all directions, the
> head is constantly spinning,
> literally and figuratively. Such was
> the case here.

and not the destination itself. We would enjoy some of
these sights the next day.

Boarding the 100-passenger tour boat, I cringed at
the tourist herd instinct but realized this was the first
time on this trip I'd been packed in with other tourists.
The ensuing beauty of the ride would more than make

up for the presence of other photo snappers and proved an understandable reason why tourists were drawn to this area. Lago Argentino allowed a four-hour ride to the Perito Moreno Glacier, the largest glacier in Argentina, in the Los Glaciares National Park. This impressive 18 mile-long glacier, fed by the Southern Patagonian Ice Field, drops dramatically into the water, leaving icebergs floating randomly about. We navigated within less than a mile of the perhaps 240-foot ice cliff, though it seemed so much closer.

There are few times in one's life when the visual sense is so impacted in all directions, the head is constantly spinning, literally and figuratively. Such was the case here. The sun shone on several acre-sized icebergs lending a clear, unusually brilliant blue color to them.

The shapes were unique and bizarre. I resisted the tourist temptation to find upside-down pianos and sideways birds in the shaped ice. They were simply exquisitely nature-crafted pieces of the glacier that had calved off as the glacier moved. I understood that most of the glaciers in this area were receding; however, this is one that, at that time, was growing. I love to imagine these valleys and lakes filled with glaciers during another age and perhaps in a future age. Man might learn some humility in the face of this kind of nature's work.

We continued to wind our way through the iceberg field, gazing at the backlit shapes. Some had holes worn from one side of the berg to the other, allowing the sun to shine through. The shapes were constantly changing, if ever so slowly. When enough mass melted in one area, the berg would shift its weight like a pregnant elephant

> The opportunities to find inspirational spots to play my pipes were endless.

moving to adjust itself. Then the full magnitude of what lay underneath these ice blocks is hinted at. The three-fourths of what is hidden will bob about and set waves in motion as the iceberg creaks to a new position.

The brilliant sun followed us to our lunch spot on an island in Lago Argentino. After dining on tasty Argentine steak in a restaurant situated by itself on this arm of the island between the peaks of Patagonia, we walked through the woods to another side of the island. This bay was also filled with more icebergs surrounded by more snow-capped, glaciated peaks.

The time was ripe for some piping. I ambled down the beach a ways to again distance myself a little from the other boat travelers. I knew this was a futile effort to remove myself from the crowd. But the appearance of not wanting to bother others was a necessary one. Of course, after the first few notes, once again the cameras focused in, and I provided a foreground feature in photos of mountains. The opportunities to find inspirational spots to play my pipes were endless.

Just as I was articulating these thoughts to myself, a man approached me with questions in his eyes. I stopped and politely explained how bagpipes worked to yet another Israeli. He reiterated my thoughts.

"Playing music in places like these is wonderful. Only then can you really feel the place. Tape recorders don't count; you must produce the music yourself."

"I agree. I guess that's one reason I've been doing this more and more on my travels."

"Yes, I had a flute that I played wherever I went. But it was stolen a few weeks ago. I really miss it."

I sympathized with his loss and played on. I could have stayed there all afternoon and more. However, the boat was leaving. I had no choice but to pack up. On the trail back to the boat, I overheard two girls speaking French. I thought I would spread some international good will and play a little of "The Marseillaise," the French anthem. But in a characteristically aloof French way, they feigned not to notice anything.

This was quite a contrast to the reaction my husband, Andrew, received at a parade our bagpipe band played in

Denver in 1987. A convention of Lions from around the world gathered in Denver, and our pipe band was invited to join the parade. Andrew, who taught French, overheard French words from the group in front of us preparing for the parade. He struck up "The Marseillaise" and was immediately swamped by Frenchmen planting kisses on his cheeks at will. It was just as well the French girls in Argentina didn't react the same way!

The boat ride back was totally peaceful to the soul. Sitting comfortably at the stern of the boat, I gazed steadily at the shrinking glacier, icebergs and peaks. The sun was slowly sinking creating an afterglow atmosphere on a place where I'd be happy to spend months, if not years.

Back on the road again, I finally gathered enough courage to sit up front next to the driver. The combination of a very large windshield and of being the first to make visual contact with another vehicle produced trepidation. But this day I knew we were approaching the Torres del Paine National Park.

This park is dominated by Cordillera del Paine, which includes three distinctive granite peaks, 2,850 meters above sea level, and just more gorgeous glaciers, mountains, lakes, and rivers! I wanted to be in the premier spot for the first views. However, I found I'd also have to watch what our bus driver was up to. After sitting on the engine cowling next to the gearshift and feeling his hand on my butt as he shifted, I realized there were more hazards to this position than I had bargained for.

Our group cheered as we re-entered Chile, equating Argentina with the nasty gritty dust. Our first views of Torres del Paine were indeed spectacular and worth the had bargained for dangers of being up front in the bus.

The Paine Towers are a unique geologic formation. The sharp, angular granitic peaks display distinct gray/black delineation. The sedimentary layer has given way to the black granite of the peaks. A fault line lies across their path creating an impressive canyon that looks up at glaciated peaks. While we were encamped in the park, a climber died during some army maneuvers. I wondered what kind of maneuvers would take them up on glaciated mountains. This has become a very popular place to hike. But on this day we experienced some quietude.

We arrived at our Quonset-style hut accommodations in time for some late afternoon walks. Now I could get away with my pipes for a needed practice without interruption. The day had smiled on us again, and the sun lent enough warmth for a pleasant walk. I strolled up a nearby knoll to yet another inspirational, awe-inspiring setting. I looked down upon a lake that appeared to reflect Chile's southern ice cap.

Mountains surrounded me; those gray/black spires contrasted sharply with the unblemished sky. The sun cast shadows in and out of the clouds, and the famous Patagonia gale had been reduced to a lovely warm gentle breeze. I rolled out all of my tunes, enjoying sending the sound into the surrounding space.

Only a few private residences existed in the national park, but the few rested within a half-mile of where I was playing my heart out. Inevitably, the children came. One black-haired boy of ten was the first to appear over the hill. He politely stood his distance and obviously enjoyed this strange break in the monotony of this remote existence.

Today, the language barrier was not an impediment. I proffered the pipes to him and set the drones on his shoulder, blow stick in his mouth and chanter in his hands. The normal awkwardness anyone feels with bagpipes the first time did not deter his enthusiasm. I let him give his best attempts as I quickly swung my camera into action. After my sought-after photo, I helped him place his fingers over the correct holes. Now, when he blew hard enough, he could make a recognizable note.

When he succeeded, his eyes bounced and lit up, warming the whole of the fading afternoon.

A brave Chilean boy gave the pipes a good effort.

More children endeavored to approach the weird sound, albeit with more circumspection than the first boy. My questions regarding sibling relationships were answered affirmatively. Their huge black eyes matched the black summits outlining their heads.

I played some more but was distracted by the littlest one of them all, characteristically hiding behind the skirts of his sister. He couldn't quite decide whether the bagpipes or I were safe, yet he was drawn to the appealing sounds. As I motioned to him to come play, he only stepped back more determinedly behind the other children.

By now, I felt comfortable enough to ask for a group photograph. Better subjects could not be found. I played more, blew myself out after a while and put my pipes away. My audience was yet again very polite and appreciative. Combined with the incredible mountain backdrop, it was a memorable experience.

I retired reluctantly to our Quonset hut with its grumbling generator. I could not describe with justice to the others what had just transpired. So I sat quietly in front of the fireplace and watched the starched, white-shirted, bow-tied, rotund and balding entrepreneur tend to his guests. He seemed to belong in Europe, in a classy alpine German or Swiss resort. He refused to blend in completely with his real setting here in the backwater of Chile and maintained a dignity worthy of great respect. To say that his excessive deference was out of place is an understatement. Yet I found his professionalism a total marvel to watch.

Our travels were winding down as we approached Punta Arenas. A side trip to the Magellanic penguin rookery at dusk was a special treat. These penguins are the only ones in the world to burrow into the ground. They are the only ones to live where the ground is soft enough to dig. Though they must have seen plenty of tourists, they were as skittish as gnats when we approached. The only way to get a really good look was to stick your head close to one of their burrows. Tales of biting beaks discouraged closer looks.

Punta Arenas was only a semblance of the town that it once was. The size of this town past its prime was surprising. Approximately 100,000 in 1987, Punta Arenas, 25 years later, had a population of 127,000. Important because of its location between the Atlantic and Pacific Oceans and the ensuing maritime trade, it began as a penal colony. But immigrants came particularly to raise sheep and for the gold rush in the late 1880s and early 1900s.

Our hotel had an impressive wall-sized mural/ photograph of the harbor around the turn of the century. Activity fairly rattled the wall with memories of pre-Panama Canal days. That morning, the sight of four lonely ships anchored in the distance past an oilrig told today's story.

The once boisterous dock area was now alive with armed soldiers guarding curious military sites. I would have loved to have lived there in its heyday. Now I was reduced to staring across the Straits of Magellan and imagining the excitement of expectant immigrants less than a century ago heading into a veritable unknown.

A huge crab dinner awash with sweet Chilean wine mellowed the crew on our last night in Chile. The next day our flight was delayed, and we spent several hours driving around the area trying to find something to do. We ended up arriving at the airport quite early, giving us ample time to generously tip our guides. I left Chile with warm feelings for the Chilanos and the country, satisfied I had left a mark with at least a few who now had heard the special sound of the Scottish Highland bagpipes.

20

I DON'T WANT TO BE IN A BAGPIPE BAND!

The tuning is exasperating enough, but there are other problems which assert themselves. Each drone has a reed, and these have personalities of their own. On any given occasion, they will blare with too much noise, or, alternatively, simply shut off with no sound.

A s I slowly walked up the stairs of Ketchum Hall on the University of Colorado campus for my first bagpipe lesson, the loud unmistakable sound of the pipes could be heard permeating the entire building. Finding the appropriate room on the third floor, therefore, was quite easy.

I entered to see my teacher, Mark, in full kilt attire, blasting away what I thought to be a great tune. I quickly learned not to refer to bagpipe music as "songs." They are tunes—pronounced "tyoons." Mark also was, at that time, the pipe major or leader of the City of Denver Bagpipe Band in Denver, Colorado.

Pipe majors for bands come and go through the years, and there had been a different pipe major that led the band in the years before Mark. Andrew Planck actually had been Mark's bagpipe teacher, and Andrew, after returning from a year living in France, would resume his position as pipe major when Mark moved to another state.

I should, at this point, make a full disclosure, which may shed light on the complete picture of my involvement with bagpipes. The pipe major before and following Mark became my husband, and we actually met in the bagpipe band! We developed a friendship, which grew for several years. I was glad I had been drawn to the pipes first and then met Andrew and not the other way around. My love of both seemed more dedicated this way.

Once the decision was made to be a piper, the next proposition I faced was whether or not to join a band. When I took the big step of signing up for my first class through the continuing education department, I had no intention whatsoever of joining a band. My visions were of a lone figure playing to the cows out in a field somewhere, far away from people.

Not only was a band not in my plans, but the very thought of joining one was absurd. I was not a joiner. I had been one of about three women in my college freshman class of several hundred not to pledge a sorority. I was not used to being part of a group and joining a band held no appeal.

Mark never really pushed the band idea on me. I just kept hearing enticing talk of all the fun they had of doing this and that gig and going to this and that place to play. He suggested I come to a band practice just to take a look, and I took him up on it. And what I saw were a lot of people having a really good time! After I had graduated from the chanter to the pipes after nine months of agonizing struggles to learn fingering, I was anxious to learn enough tunes to

> They are driven to maintain rationality in the face of total frustration with an instrument that defies all the laws of sanity.

become an accepted member of his band. Little did I know that this decision would change my life!

How can I describe what it's like to be a member of a bagpipe band? Though I have never been a part of another band, I discovered that bagpipes lent uniqueness to our camaraderie. Don't let anyone kid you; bagpipers have to be demented to some degree. This element of craziness must be what holds bagpipe bands together.

Except for the common interest in bagpiping, the individuals comprising bagpipe bands are a very curious lot. Professions of the members of my band were as varied as the different uniforms you can see on bagpipers. Teachers, carpenters, bureaucrats, craftsmen, airline pilots, editors, students, a TV weatherman, out-of-work sponges on society, and computer analysts sound like any cross-section of society.

Our band consisted of 20 some pipers, fewer than ten drummers, and a hodge-podge of Scottish Highland and Irish dancers all managing to find some form of satisfaction in being part of a bagpipe band. Get these people around bagpipes and a metamorphosis takes place. These otherwise normal people shed all trappings of regular life and become semi-maniacal. They are driven to maintain rationality in the face of total frustration with an instrument that defies all the laws of sanity.

This common, intermittent leave of the senses creates a bond that the outside world has difficulty comprehending. In spite of our wide differences, we generally enjoyed each other socially. I think we all looked at each other with some incredulity while appreciating each other's tolerance for our own idiosyncrasies.

Why else would we put up with a past pipe major who always greedily lusted after every crumb left on a table of well devoured chicken dinners? Even after we piled our gnawed-on chicken bones on his plate and watched him scarf the tidbits down, we still continued to associate with him. And why did we put up with a teacher of incorrigible teenagers who were in prison, who never caught an announcement the first time, and who always asked the question that had just been answered?

On the other hand, why did the piper who, every week, traveled two hours from Wyoming to Denver for practices put up with our teasing him about his sheep relatives? He should have run to the nearest exit. We not only tolerated one another, we thrived on this bizarre form of support group.

The ages in the band varied from 15 to more than 70, and the amount of bagpipe experience varied accordingly. Aspiring pipers came and went regularly. After five or ten lessons, the dedication and stubbornness it takes to graduate from chanter to the pipes can become discouragingly apparent, and many pipers-to-be give up the effort.

I suppose we all have different reasons for having stuck with this insane instrument. But basically, we were all attracted to the unique sound of the pipes. I know of few other instruments that so many people begin to learn when they are "older." Forty year olds are commonly found to be taking chanter in hand for the first time and devoting countless hours developing the fingering techniques.

I've wondered why so many older people who should know better attempt to learn bagpiping. I have inconclusively decided that the time-is-running-out syndrome for people who "have always wanted to play bagpipes" is greater than the price for a set of pipes. Perhaps, even the midlife crisis thing sneaks in, and pipes provide a satisfaction that being a successful yuppie couldn't fulfill.

Most of the band members developed nicknames, which went on their uniform nametags. As a rule, the individual had no say in the matter. My first gig with the band earned my nickname, which, in spite of my hopes that the incident would quickly fade from memory, remained on my nametag for 15 years. A take-out pizza parlor had hired the band to draw attention to its grand opening. With no space in the pizza parlor to play, we were forced out onto the parking lot to fight the elements of a cold, wet March.

While standing in our requisite circle playing the first set of tunes, I was terribly nervous, unsure, and uncomfortable in what seemed a ridiculous outfit. In all my anticipation, I failed to notice I was standing in a puddle of melted snow. When this was brought to my attention, the word "Puddles" jumped out from one piper's mouth. Eliciting much mirth from the group, I tried to act nonchalant and dismissed it as some initiation rite.

However, later in the afternoon, as we were warming up at a drummer's house, his cat spilled my beer to form a puddle under my feet, while I was sitting innocently in a corner. Of course the incident didn't go unnoticed, and shortly after that I was presented with my band nametag, which had "Puddles" emblazoned on it.

Pipers can get tired of explaining some of these names. "Ex-lax" was the nickname given to a gifted piper, Rob, who moved very quickly from one grade to another in competition. Some pipers languish in the lowest grade, grade IV, all of their competition lives. Many manage to improve to Grade III and others even to Grades II and I after many years if they are very talented. Rob found himself in Grade II in less than three years of playing. The quick slide into that grade produced the nickname and gave him headaches explaining it ever since.

Andrew, who taught French was known as "L'état, c'est moi," or "I am the state," roughly meaning, I am the big cheese, while he was pipe major. Another innocent piper learned a nice march, which vaguely sounded like the children's song, "I'm a Little Teapot, short and stout …." His band name became "Little Teapot."

The best nickname may have been earned by one of our more well endowed dancers. While grabbing food in a buffet, she casually reached over a tray to add some food to her plate. A band member ahead of her had some chicken noodle soup on the tray that happened to be in the way. The dancer ended up with soup on her boob, resulting in her nickname of "Chicken Nipple."

One of the band's favorite jokes to play on people was a bit crude, which is exactly why the band enjoyed it so much. The unsuspecting receiver of this antic is told:

"We have just read about a scientific study done on the Chesapeake Bay oysters. A team of researchers spent many years studying the mating call of these oysters, and we have practiced their intricate ritual."

The band, at this point, hides their heads behind their folded arms, waiting for the signal. At the appointed time, arms open to approximate oyster shells opening, heads peek out between the arms, and, in unison, all cry out, "Wanna fuck?" Laughter follows, at least from the band. The victims have been known to have various other responses.

21

DOWN HOME IN COLORADO

With my heart beating hard in my chest in great anticipation of establishing a psychic rapport with an elk, I gave a strong toot on the pipe's chanter—no drones, no tune, just one long meaningful note.

One common perception about bagpipe bands is that they promote and foster drunken rowdiness. There does seem to be a correlation between piping and drinking. After all, Scotland is the home of Scotch whiskey and bagpipes. After piping in 40° F. drizzle all day on the Highlands of

Scotland or in a mile-long parade in Denver, a wee dram is very welcome.

My band was a study in contrasts regarding the booze scene. My first pipe major enjoyed drinking as much as anyone, and the band followed his lead. Stories abound about past road trips that involved motel lobbies awash with swimming pool water, and swimming suits that have disappeared in pools. And those motels have been careful not to invite the band back.

A transformation in our drinking habits took place with a changing of the guard and Andrew Planck was reinstalled as pipe major. Andrew initiated a rule that no drinking of any kind would take place before a performance. Amidst some grumbling from some but gratitude from many others, the band made a complete turnaround in a year. At first, people found it strange not to have a few drinks before a performance. As time went on, however, we knew that the quality of our piping gigs had improved perceptibly and pride multiplied. When we saved our celebrations for afterward, moderation seemed natural.

More people hear pipes in a parade than anywhere else. I suppose that is where I first became enamored with their sound, though the exact time and place escapes me. And parades, though they can become commonplace to pipers, cause such elation from the crowds that pipers will brave all sorts of elements to please the masses.

Some parades are obviously better than others. Not all take place on bright, warm sunny days. The St. Patrick's Day Parade of 1988 in Denver would have tested the metal of even a true Scot. With a temperature of less than 20°F. and a 15 mph wind, even the diehards among us decided not to go "regimental."

Denver claims to have one of the largest St. Paddy's Day parades in the country. Although delays are common before parades, and acceptable on good days, the delay in our start caused by the large size of the parade thoroughly numbed toes, noses, and, more importantly to a piper, fingers. Gloves simply don't work. Our fingers froze as well as drone reeds, chanter reeds, and everything else.

My problem was my mouth. I could not get a seal around the mouthpiece. I believe I marched the whole parade without getting one sound out of the chanter! The drones played on wobbly enough, but hypothermia was on my mind.

Somehow we finished the parade. Fortunately, others in the band weren't so wimpy, and we produced enough sound for the intrepid bystanders who braved the cold to celebrate the Irish. Afterward, we quickly retired to a nearby bar to thaw ourselves, eat and warm our gullets a bit.

This proved to be no ordinary meal, for, in the corner with a suitable entourage, was Senator Gary Hart who had pulled out of the Democratic presidential primaries only a few months before because of an illicit liaison. Nothing would do but that we would play for him. Even our dancers would contribute. We launched into a few sets and embarked on one of our livelier tunes for a hornpipe dance. Gary Hart and friends seemed suitably impressed, and we retired to the comfort of the booths and food.

At that point, a realization dawned on us. Unfortunately, the dance tune we had played for Senator Hart was called "The Clumsy Lover," and one of the pipers, once he realized the coincidence, mentioned it out loud. As luck would have it, a newspaper reporter overheard the comment and published it in the next day's paper. Andrew, our pipe major, was chagrined and wrote a letter of apology to Senator Hart explaining that it was a standard tune that we had been playing all day and no harm was intended. We were graced with a reply stating, "If that is the worst I receive in the press, I wouldn't be much of a politician."

Our parade experience would only get more interesting the next day in Colorado Springs. The cold wave continued in Colorado, and we prepared with winter underwear and fingerless gloves, which also didn't work very well. What we failed to predict was a snowfall during our marching. Undaunted, we finished the parade to empty streets, while two inches of snow piled on our epaulets and hats and matted in the beards of our players. We were a good match for any abominable snowman.

We were a crazy lot!

Shortly after that, I missed the coldest parade in the band's memory. I was off skiing like any sensible person would be when snow hits Colorado. The rest of the band would regret being available for the Denver Broncos football team welcome-home parade after one of their losses in the Super Bowl. The wind chill was more than minus 10° F. In spite of the cold, our business manager had thought the publicity warranted a free performance with the Broncos. Frozen appendages afterward told him otherwise. We were a crazy lot!

And we do this sort of thing for fun. Bands are totally voluntary. Any money earned went to the band, not any individuals, to pay for uniforms, travel and some supplies, though pipers and drummers expend plenty of their own money. The uniforms are no simple matter. A kilt, tunic, belt, cross belt, Glengarry hat, two pairs of hose or knee socks with flashes to hold them up, a horsehair sporran or leather sporran, depending on the formality of occasion, and shirt cost more than $1,000 per person.

Some bands will just use a dress coat instead of a complicated tunic, but the individual usually pays for that. Players buy their own shoes and pipes. Struggling into this outfit for the first time was so unnerving, I had to call my pipe major to ask how it all went together.

Kilts are actually a male item of clothing. Females didn't start to wear them until the twentieth century. Pipes weren't played by women much before then either. And even now, there may be some bands that don't accept women—as well as women bands that don't accept men.

In contrast to these less enjoyable parades in freezing weather is the annual St. Patrick's Day parade in 10,000 foot high Leadville, Colorado, which is held in the middle of September. March 17, the real St. Patrick's Day, is intolerably cold and snowy at this altitude in Colorado. So, the city managers plan the St. Paddy's Day parade for the middle of September, usually a beautiful time of year there.

This parade has real character and chutzpah. A town of fewer than 3,000 cannot afford to bring in too many bands. In fact, along with the mayor and one fire truck, we were the parade. We would march, huffing and puffing at this altitude, five blocks down one side of the street and then march, huffing and puffing, five blocks back up the other side of the street. We then would pour ourselves into the historic Irish pub near the end of the street. One of the stipulations of our attendance was that we not go into the bar across the street. Some people apparently don't always appreciate our exuberance.

Church gigs, on the other hand, can be quite impressive and more appropriate for bagpipes. Organ and bagpipe is a dynamite combination. This was clearly the case during a Presbyterian Church convention in Denver's Coliseum one year. The ties between Scotland and the Presbyterian Church are well known. We were asked to play the introduction and the finale of their Sunday festivities. Though it was a long wait until the finale, we knew it would be worth it.

Everyone is familiar with "Amazing Grace." It's a bit overplayed at functions like these. We chose a tune not so well known. "Highland Cathedral" is similar in mood but even more moving and inspirational. We gave a copy of the music to the music director, John Kuzma, who was also an internationally known composer, conductor and orchestrator. John set about composing additional parts for organ, brass ensemble and chorus. The result was positively bewitching.

After the lengthy service ended, Andrew began to play the solo introduction to the finale. People who had been sitting a bit too long started to leave and pour into the walkways. Then the rest of the bagpipes and the organ joined the solo piper and the exodus slowed. When the brass band joined in with the organ, people quieted, stopped and sat down. Then the crowning glory, the 100-person choir, rose in song and tears flowed freely from every eye in the house. The crash of a huge Chinese gong at the appropriate moment added to the total splendor of the performance.

All of us were so overwhelmed by the power and the majesty of the music that it was difficult to continue, but we managed. The combination of pipes, organ, brass ensemble, and 100-voice chorus was the single most powerful musical experience any of us had ever had and will be forever burned in our memories.

Most bagpipe gigs are more mundane and what you might expect. Bagpipes and bars are a natural combination. Particularly near St. Patrick's Day, the band braces for less than discerning audiences. The Irish tradition is alive and well across the country. An Irish heritage magically surfaces where it has been unacknowledged before. Suddenly everyone is telling you about his or her great-grandmother and long lost uncle from Ireland.

Marching into a bar in downtown Denver, our bagpipe band entertained the noonday St. Patrick's Day crowd every year. At this time of the day the crowd is manageable and appreciative. Discussions following the performance focus on the usual Irish-Scottish background and on the whys and wherefores of bagpipe playing.

By the second show at 2 p.m., patronage has enjoyed the green beer for a bit longer and has swollen in numbers making it difficult to navigate through the bar playing our pipes. Now discussions centered on what we wore under our kilts. The third and fourth shows were just plain brute survival. We spent less time tuning with a full realization that the crowd barely knew the difference between bagpipes and saxophones by then. Negotiating the route through the bar had become all but impossible, yet we somehow found a spot to play a few tunes and let the dancers show their stuff.

But I still had this idea of playing out in a meadow just for myself, doing the communing-with-nature thing. One fall day, I found myself camping in Rocky Mountain National Park. My primary objective in the evening was to search out the elk that were in rutting season. The bugle of a bull elk desperately trying to attract a mate is one of God's greatest sounds. There is none other like it. Halfway between a scratchy whine of a trumpet and a grunt of an elephant, the sound is pure sex. The call leaves no doubt as to its purpose. I was curious to know if an elk would respond to a single note on the bagpipe sans drones in a similar way deer had in other places I tried. I had visions of "taming the wild elk."

During the mating season, the elk become emboldened and wander down from the remote hills to the valleys in herds. The casual tourist can drive around the Park and encounter elk by the roadside with no trouble at all. In fact, you can golf with them at the right time of year. Elk will congregate on the luscious fairways of golf courses in Estes Park, awash with gratitude for their good fortune at finding such tasty grass.

The lure of listening to bugling elk has become incredibly strong and popular. At night when activity for elk and cars is at its peak, visitors frequently produce major traffic jams. Car lights and people noise have all but destroyed the idyllic scene and muffled the primordial sound of a rutting elk. Still, I was able to find a remote cul-de-sac with elk grazing close by the road.

In the growing dusk of evening, I saw one, which was faintly silhouetted 20 yards away. I slowly slipped my pipes out of the trunk of the car, being careful not to draw attention to myself. With my heart beating hard in my chest in great anticipation of establishing a psychic rapport with an elk, I gave a strong toot on the pipe's chanter—no drones, no tune, just one long meaningful note.

I pulled the chanter to one side and anxiously squinted into the murky dark. Not only was I not being attacked, the elk had not even raised its head from eating! Disappointed but not deterred, I gave the chanter another shot. I played two notes this time and tried to put some feeling into it—still nothing. My heart's beating had now slowed somewhat, but I was not dissuaded.

More efforts of communicating with the elk produced total and absolute indifference. I walked closer. A magnificent elk minding his own business chomping away on the tasty grass, while some strange figure with three sticks over a shoulder and a bulky object under an arm tiptoeing closer and closer, should have at least looked up in consternation. Nothing … until finally the elk decided there was something bizarre happening but "it" wasn't a female elk. The bull elk trotted off absent-mindedly into the dark. I had failed and felt the rejection some of the bull elk were feeling that night—

but in a different sense, to be sure. Elk aren't dumb. At least one had had no trouble telling the difference between a bagpiper and a female elk.

Later that year I would take the classic ski vacation to Steamboat Springs, Colorado. One of the premier ski towns in the country, Steamboat offers some of the best skiing in Colorado. My sister from Wisconsin had joined me, and we skied with a vengeance. The late February days were unseasonably warm, even hot on this particular day. At 60°F., the day, under the intense sun on snow, felt more like 80°F.

Finally, after more than 30 years of skiing, I realized that this was my chance to ski in a bathing suit. I had seen many photos of gals strutting their stuff on skis, but I had never really skied in what I deemed bathing suit weather. Today was the day!

As I pulled on my suit that morning, I reflected on those official ski area photographers stationed at the mid-mountain restaurant. As long as I was going to risk the bathing suit scene, why not add a little pizzazz to it all? Why not take my bagpipes along?

I could foresee logistical problems. Although my pipes fit pretty well in my daypack, I didn't want to ski cautiously all day fearing a fall on the pipes on my back. I figured I could stash them in a locker, ski the morning, and return to the locker for lunch and see about stripping off my ski clothes down to the bathing suit for some piping.

All morning on the slopes I fretted about the impending scene. Wouldn't this be a bit too exhibitionist? This wasn't something I could do on the sly. When the time came, the urge to back out was intense. But I checked the pipes out of the locker and made my way quickly to a photographer before I regained my senses and ducked out of the whole thing.

I told the photographer what I was about to do, and at the same time, saw that I could coax him away from the front of the gondola house down a rise out of the glaring eyes of everyone disembarking from the gondola. He was amenable and followed me 75 yards away.

I quickly stripped down to the suit. Though having to remove skis and boots in order to remove ski pants didn't make the procedure very speedy. While my sister held my clothes in disbelief, I set up the pipes and prayed they wouldn't be too badly out of tune. The photographer finally started to get the idea. Bathing suits he'd seen before; pipes were perhaps a first.

Of course, the very first note brought over a large crowd that I'd taken pains to avoid. The official photographer's camera wasn't the only one in action now. After playing "Amazing Grace" as a request from an onlooker, I was ready to pack up. It was then a fellow from the crowd stepped forward suggesting others show similar appreciation for the music as he stuffed a dollar bill down my suit! Time to move on! Then I realized it was actually more pleasant to ski in the suit rather than with all of those ski clothes. I stuffed the pipes and the clothes in the pack, realizing I would have to ski carefully to avoid a crash if I fell anyway, and took off down the hill. A

good day was had. I would try the bagpiping skier act again at Snowmass, but it wasn't as warm and sunny. And there's nothing like the first time!

I finally got to ski in a bathing suit!

22
BAGPIPES IN NEBRASKA AND TENNESSEE?

Having an opportunity to introduce bagpipes to those who rarely hear them and eliciting such favorable responses is an incomparable joy. Sidney liked us and we liked the town. Bagpipes and Nebraska, why not!

Not all piping is performed in parades. Bagpipe bands are called upon for all sorts of affairs, from weddings and funerals to fairs and church functions, supermarket openings, and even a Monday Night Football game. Then Sidney, Nebraska, discovered us for its Oktoberfest. Sidney is a role model for Nebraska towns in its simplicity and honesty and is surrounded by nothing but cornfields.

The town itself could be Anywhere, USA, with 6,000 or so inhabitants trying to make a go of life in Middle America. The one main street in the 1990s was filled with the basic necessity stores: a drug store, Penny's, Radio Shack, a local hardware enterprise, and several empty storefronts, advertising a town that was not as prosperous as it once had been. In spite of a large Cabella's store employing more than 2,000 workers, Sidney's focus was probably on its high school football team.

The Oktoberfest at the end of September in Sidney was one of the biggest events of the year. A huge tent of circus proportions was erected in the park, and most of the town and visitors fit under it. Visitors would come from clear across the state or even several states away.

Everyone seemed to have a good time, albeit perhaps a bit of a drunken one. Different musical acts entertained the locals as the day progressed into the evening. The German theme of an Oktoberfest was all but ignored, and anything from clogging (dances that originated in Europe, done with special wooden shoes) to country-western duets to bagpipe bands could be heard.

Our first performance in the evening was usually a
real crowd awakening. We entered the tent, pipes roaring
and kilts swaying. I don't think many, if any, Sidney folks
had been exposed to bagpipes before. Incredulous looks
accompanied pleased smiles as we marched to the center
stage. Our dancers attracted much of the admiration,
yet, the entire band made a huge impact on the crowd.
As we concluded our foray into Middle America and
beat a retreat after playing several sets of tunes, one old-
timer was somehow heard over the cacophony. Toothless
and probably hard of hearing, the great grandfather of
the crowd turned to his wife of 53 years and said, "You
know, Maud, I think I might get to like this here music."
Success!

Having an opportunity to introduce bagpipes to
those who rarely hear them and eliciting such favorable
responses is an incomparable joy. Sidney liked us and we
liked the town. Bagpipes and Nebraska, why not! We
would be invited back to Sidney for more than 30 years
running! I believe it is the only time I have been asked for
my autograph!

Memphis, Tennessee, would be another strange
marriage of our band and local uncertainly about
bagpipes. Memphis holds a highly successful annual civic
affair every spring called "Memphis in May." The planners

celebrate a different country and culture every year. The highlights of the week's events are the performances in the coliseum on Friday and Saturday nights.

In 1988, "Memphis in May" focused on the United Kingdom. Our prior pipe major, Mark, had moved to Arkansas a couple of years earlier to manage a Scottish Studies Program at a college in nearby Batesville. While involved in the Scottish community in Memphis, he had heard that the organizers of the festival were looking for a bagpipe band. Of course, he thought of his old band back in Denver and suggested us to the organizers. Besides, he was looking forward to possibly playing with us in the performances.

Wheels were put in motion, and our band was sent tickets to fly to Memphis and represent the Scottish tradition of the British Isles. The Irish Guards, a well-regarded bagpipe band from Ireland, would also send a contingent of pipers. Other bands would include the Marine Brass Band, the Barbados Brass Band and others. The night's entertainment even included an American Indian dance contingent. The connection to things British was lost on us unless someone was thinking of the French and Indian War or something of the sort.

Otherwise, we were in high-powered company and felt the pressure keenly. The truth was we were out of our element. The other bands were professionals, tried and true—experienced performers. We were just "a bunch of rag-tailed civilians," according to one member of the band.

The official welcoming committee of the "Memphis in May" celebration met us as we arrived at Memphis Airport. Arrangements had been made for us to stay in private homes. Residents who had been hosts previously with other groups visiting Memphis had parceled us out and took us directly to our first practice.

We ran into the Marine Band right away, thanks in part to a 16-year-old cutie of a dancer, the daughter of one of our pipers, who seemed to attract a lot of attention. Also, several members of the band had been in the Marine Corps. The Marines were friendly folks and felt a kinship with the pipe major who displayed some Marine Corps medals on his band uniform, and they apparently enjoyed the uniqueness of meeting a bagpipe band up close and personal.

At age 41, I felt almost like a grandmother to these young jarheads with the shaven heads. My reaction as a female at this time in my life was total disinterest, but there was one curious incident. Our bands were entertained with a ride in a sternwheeler down the Mississippi River the next morning, and friendships among pipers, dancers and Marines formed. Standing an aloof distance away, enjoying the scenery, I was focusing on the upcoming performances. Our 23-year-old attractive female piper, who had also gathered her share of the Marines' attention, tapped me on the shoulder. One of the Marines wanted to meet me.

"How desperate can this guy be?" I wondered, as I unenthusiastically moseyed over to the group. This was before Andrew and I had formed a special bond. The fellow was all smiles, and we were formally introduced. After some small talk, I drifted away figuring he'd be satisfied now that he had gotten a better idea of my age and disinterest. Never underestimate the Marines!

More small talk was to be had before that evening's performance. When he told me he thought I was one of the most beautiful women he had seen, I should have thanked him and felt complimented. Instead, I passed it off as a lame line and moved away. I laughed it off to myself—until later.

We all retired to the hotel bar across the street after the show in a self-congratulatory celebration. The first night had gone well, and we deserved a pat on the back. Before I could settle into my first beer, here was the not bad-looking, young Marine settling in next to me.

This time the small talk moved quickly to his hobby. Without much ado and with some apparent pride, he proceeded to tell me that he was a stripper in his spare time! This certainly was a new slant on the Marines I hadn't seen before. I have to say, his comment did manage to pique my interest.

"Where did you learn to do this?" I asked. "Do the Marines know you do this? Where do you—uh—perform? Why do you like to strip?"

He answered in a straightforward manner without embarrassment. Then he suggested what I should have known was coming.

He wore a bikini-type brief and probably some kind of shirt, though I admit to not remembering the shirt.

"Why don't you come up to my room, and I'll give you a demonstration?"

Now I had to admit to being embarrassed. Just exactly what would I see? More importantly, what would I do? I was somewhat pleased that a 27-year-old Marine would want an old lady of 41 in his room to watch a strip act. My curiosity got the best of me. Besides I knew it would make a good story to tell the band later.

Reluctantly and with much trepidation, I followed him up to his hotel room. Upon entering, he set up his tape machine and retired into the bathroom to get his "costume" on. Meanwhile, I sat nervously on the bed wondering if I was getting myself into trouble.

After what seemed an unusually long time, I was directed to start the music as he entered. He wore a bikini-type brief and probably some kind of shirt, though I admit to not remembering the shirt. He proceeded to dance to the music as I watched totally perplexed. As he took off the first briefs down to a skimpier pair, I started to chuckle, finding the whole scene pretty amusing. Looking back, I don't know if this reaction insulted him or not; I have no idea what reaction I was supposed to have. I certainly did not feel turned on to such a bodacious display of overt sexuality.

He continued to dance to the music and took off the second pair of briefs. I was sure there couldn't be anything underneath, but to my relief there was. And my chuckle erupted into laughter, no doubt more out of nervousness than anything else, though I did find it all quite amusing.

At this point, I didn't have a clue what his next step would be, nor did I want to find out. I think he must have felt my uneasiness and stopped the show. Whether or not he got a special high performing for me, I'll never

know. I thanked him, told him he did a good job, and
bolted for the door.

I returned to the bar having enjoyed my experience
but relieved to be back in the safety of the band. As I was
locating my local hosts preparing to leave, my Marine
friend returned to the bar in civvies appearing none
the worse. As I was introducing him to my friends, he
presented me with some gifts. A Marine t-shirt was a real
bonus, but he actually gave me a pair of his strip briefs!
What in hell was I going to do with that? My hosts who
were set to drive me back to their home for the night
provided a good excuse to slip out the door.

Memphis was an eye-opener for me. I was surprised to
find that racism was still alive and well in 1988. Some of
our host families had no compunctions about expressing
their racism openly to us, assuming that we would be in
complete agreement. I had never heard the word "nigger"
spat out about an African-American before.

The town seemed to be trying to figure out its
character. Famous for Elvis Presley's Graceland estate and
Martin Luther King's shooting site, Memphis still boasts
Beale Street and the Blues. Less than two hours away
was the Civil War battlefield of Shiloh in Mississippi,
which a few of the band members were able to visit. I
was definitely in "The South," and people there would be

sure that I wouldn't forget it. Yet I played my bagpipes there and gave them something to think about, too.

We got in two or three practices before the show had been scheduled. Initially, instructions bellowed in the arena were unclear, confusing and garbled at best. Our band was convinced that this show would never come together for a credible performance. Bands were playing in different keys and/or playing the same tunes but using different versions. The captain of the Irish Guards was singularly uncommunicative and apparently seething that his group had to be associated with an amateur band from the colonies.

One bright light was Captain James McFarland. A captain in the British military, he was a member of the Scots Guards and was brought over from the Edinburgh Tattoo to run the show in Memphis. He was miraculous at producing a successful event.

In the 18th century, the term Tattoo came to mean not just the last duty call of the day, but a ceremonial form of entertainment performed by military musicians. Today, nightly Tattoos are performed beneath Edinburgh Castle for several weeks every August. The Tattoo attracts thousands of visitors from around the world to see bagpipe bands, dancers, and other spectacular musical presentations in wonderful precision.

At first, we guffawed at what seemed a parody on the British approach and language. Captain McFarland's British accent was so strong, we thought it was totally affected and unreal. But, shouting directions from a podium in the other end of the coliseum, he commanded attention and seemed utterly professional. His prowess at organizing such an event became quickly evident.

My band was to have one solo act and appear two other times, once with the Irish Guards and once at the finale with everyone. Our solo went well, and the audience was extremely warm and receptive. As the evening wore on, the audience was getting into the feel of a traditional "tattoo" and became more animated and enthusiastic.

By the time the finale came, they were ripe to be plucked. All the bands marched in, filling the entire stadium floor of the 6,000 person capacity coliseum. We were the last to march in at the rear of the entire entourage. After the requisite final tunes played by all, including "Auld Lang Syne," the bands marched off together as a wave, all except us.

We remained standing until the floor was clear. At the appropriate command, we struck up the rousing "Black Bear," and strode across the entire arena by ourselves. Instantly, the entire audience rose to their feet in tumultuous applause. We were the darlings of Memphis that night and new pride and confidence were instilled in our band.

23

ARE COMPETITIONS ANY FUN?

Inspired by the 1960s movie "Zulu," Andrew had improvised a version of a Zulu chant for the band to yell during moments of victory. It was a gloriously "in your face" chant that we would yell whenever we got first place. To the uninitiated, Scottish bagpipe band members screaming Zulu war chants at the top of their lungs might have seemed a bit strange.

Competing as a member of a bagpipe band, or even competing as a solo bagpiper, gives special meaning to the word competition. I suppose I have always had the competitive spirit whether it was grade school baseball games or playing a game of Scrabble or Trivial Pursuit between fellow teachers during our abbreviated lunch breaks. I was out to win. As I grew older, the spirit remained but the opportunities to test the competitiveness became fewer.

Then I found myself not only in a bagpipe band but one that traveled to Highland games throughout the United States to compete against other bands. As long as the band was going to compete, I figured I might as well become totally masochistic and compete as a solo player, too.

Competition is like jogging or hitting your head against the wall; it feels so good when you stop. I always experienced a wave of immense relief after finishing a tune—and pride that I had the guts to try, even though opportunities of making a fool of myself were innumerable. I felt a definite rush after playing for a piping judge.

The fact that I had enjoyed some success helped add some appeal to solo competition. Winning never hurts, "It's not whether you win or lose, it is how you play the game" notwithstanding. Winning is nice, though it really is not the only thing, in spite of what Green Bay Packer's coach, Vince Lombardi, said. Sometimes I found myself actually enjoying the tunes I played during competition.

General nervousness creates sweaty hands and shortness of breath. These are two deadly enemies of a piper. An Olympic diver can have sweaty palms and still splash into the water correctly. A racecar driver can have short breaths and still drive his car to victory. Adrenaline has helped many a competitor.

However, a piper who suffers too much adrenaline over-blows and his pipes sound out of tune. Sweaty fingers slip and slide over wrong holes producing wrong notes. Shortness of breath makes the drones sound wobbly. As if playing pipes wasn't hard enough, competition further complicates a difficult instrument.

Preparation for competition is particularly unnerving. The first step is to play the pipes in private to "settle them in." Warming them up takes maybe a half hour of playing, yet you can't blow too much or you "blow yourself out." You need enough air to keep blowing because now it's time to tune them. The chanter itself needs to have the right sound. Even though there are only nine notes, the octave must be accurate, and the whole sound should not be too flat or too sharp. The reed can be moved in or out to accomplish this, but a good ear is needed to determine which direction to go and how far. And this good ear may or may not be developed over time. So, as a result, beginners who haven't yet developed this ear try to grab experienced players to have them tune their pipes.

After the chanter reed is set, the drones need attending to. They're somewhat easier to tune. They have slides to effect different pitches. The two tenor drones should be set at the same tone, an octave lower than the low A on the chanter; the base drone is one octave lower than that. The problems come when the tone changes as the pipes are played. This can be due either to moisture, heat, cold, unsteady blowing, or just the phases of the moon.

Sometimes they never settle down and stay in tune. I saw one professional player tune his pipes for fifteen minutes in front of a judge only to have the drones go out of tune in the first bar and get progressively worse as the long tune progressed. At the end of the piece, he actually threw his irreplaceable pipes on the ground and apologized to the judge for putting him through such agony.

The tuning is exasperating enough, but there are other problems which assert themselves. Each drone has a reed, and these have personalities of their own. On any given occasion, they will blare with too much noise, or, alternatively, simply shut off with no sound. Reeds may drop into the bag with potentially embarrassing, even disastrous, results. Every piper at one time in his career has picked up the pipes only to find he can't get air into the bag. A reed lost in a bag allows air to escape unimpeded through the drone. The piper must then awkwardly crouch over the pipes on the ground and feel around the bag until he locates the errant reed. He must then jockey it to the drone and reseat it.

Once the reeds are set, the piper is presumably ready to compete. Approaching the judge seated in sartorial elegance at a table, he presents the name of the tune and is given an opportunity for last minute tuning. He takes a deep breath, does some fine-tuning, and finally launches into the tune.

It may be at this exact time a drone chooses to go out. Pop! It's gone. No sound from the drone. The judge's head jerks up, the piper is startled and goes off the tune, and another fine effort is down the tubes. An important trick is to soldier on no matter what. Something worse may happen to your competitors, and pipers have even won some competitions missing a drone. But some judges immediately disqualify the competitor. Such is the temperament of the pipes, pipers and judges. We do this for fun! I keep reminding myself that I subjected myself to all this masochism voluntarily.

I am convinced that there are cosmic factors affecting bagpiping other than just ability and the pipes themselves.

Once two other band members and I competed as a trio. We hadn't practiced much, and the weather was typically Scottish—cold, wet and generally dismal. Our pipes had exhibited schizophrenic personalities all day.

It was after 3 p.m. when we finally approached the judge. We were exhausted from all our solo competitions as well as two band competitions. And there had been a "massed bands" presentation where all the bands at the games marched onto the field at noon playing common tunes. Between the cold, clammy weather, exhaustion, and fluky pipes, our dedication and concentration were lacking.

We shrugged our shoulders and dove into our three-minute medley of several tunes. Immediately, I realized I had only one drone working. I wasn't sure, but I didn't hear much from the others' drones either. Our chanter work managed to stay on track, and we charged through the lively tunes without too many mistakes. As we trudged off the field, we shared our frustrations and realized each of us had had only one drone, enough for one set of bagpipes! Ironically, we managed to get first place! The other trios apparently had experienced more trouble than we had.

The "thrill of victory" is a special feeling, especially when shared with your band. My first two years competing with the band were frustrating. We were struggling due to general band politics and temporary setbacks. By my third year, we were loaded for bear. Our normal one-day a week practice had extended into Friday nights as well. The twelve pipers and five drummers in the competition band could smell blood. We knew we had a chance at some prizes.

ALBUQUERQUE, NEW MEXICO

Our first opportunity came in Albuquerque, New Mexico—not what one might expect as a hotbed of bagpiping. But Albuquerque does have an active Scottish community that sponsored a small Highland games. We carpooled the eight-hour drive and shared rooms at the less than expansive Motel 6.

Arriving Friday afternoon, we arranged to gather on the field of battle that evening for one last practice before our first test. As the bright classic New Mexico sun set behind threatening black thunderheads, we marched back and forth practicing the finer points of our presentation. More than anything, I think we were working out the butterflies.

All of our efforts paid off the next day. With only three other bands to contend with, we won with apparent ease. Still, the first victory was more than gratifying. We had picked ourselves up after a season in which we had found ourselves only as observers because we lacked the required number of drummers. Now we had a good start to the season as top dogs. The drive home is a lot sweeter with a victory behind you.

In later years, we decided to splurge a bit and stay at nicer places, especially if they had pools, hot tubs, and a liberal happy hour. We certainly gave hot tubs a test for the number of people who can fit in.

Then there was the year we were bouncing a beach ball around in a circle in the pool. With a beer or two under our belts, somehow—I cannot remember the details, no matter how hard I try—I became the ball, only to be tossed from one member to another. This went on until I had gulped so much water I was on the verge of drowning. Unfortunately, it subsequently became a popular band sport known as "Susan ball."

After our victory in Albuquerque, reality slowly returned and our enthusiasm for the upcoming season was tempered by a little humility. Our competition in New Mexico had not been big name stuff. We had to find another Highland games, which attracted other bands with proven track records. And it had to be soon, while we were still "peaking." It's a long distance from

Colorado to anywhere with a Highland games. We had a choice between California and Texas. California offered more prize money and free lodging. So off to Vallejo we flew.

GOLDEN GATE AND SANTA ROSA, CALIFORNIA

A prettier spot with nicer weather would be hard to find. The fairgrounds offered lots of shade—a welcome cover from the pipe's enemy, the sun. Small but well managed, the Golden Gate Games in Vallejo had an organizer who was trying to establish these games as a major event in the West.

Sadly, this would be his only Games. To his disappointment and ours, many bands, which had indicated they were coming, did not appear. Again, we were to have only three competitive bands. Their quality pushed us a bit more, but we came away with three out of four wins.

The season would see three more major competitions, two in Colorado and the big one in Santa Rosa, California. Feeling pretty cocky, we still realized that the games in Santa Rosa would have eight or more bands in our grade IV, but we were hyped and ready. Bands are put in a certain grade, depending on their level of playing. Grade I bands are the best; Grade IV are the lower level bands, though in some areas the pipe band associations even have Grade V bands.

Duly impressed by the Canadian Grade I and II bands, we had no illusions about ourselves. We would have to play better than ever to win. Each one of us concentrated on the task. Besides wanting to have fun on the trip in general, we also wanted to win.

The intensity of tuning up one hour prior to competition is beyond comprehension. The nerve-wracking lowering and raising of the chanter reed to be in tune with the other pipes is a continuous back and forth process. Nervousness can be displayed as anger, and memory lapses for tunes are common. Concern about arriving at the competition circle at the appropriate time increases; a late arrival means disqualification. Palms are increasingly sweaty.

Still, fine-tuning stretches on, and the music is practiced once more. The walk from the tuning area to the performing area is done hurriedly; waiting too long at the entrance of the area increases agitation as well as the likelihood of the pipes changing their tuning. Finally we were announced. Incredibly, as soon as we struck up and marched off into the judge's lair, I felt relieved and combative.

Competing with a band is different from competing solo. With a band, there is pressure not to screw up and hurt the others in the band, but there is an overwhelming sense of support, too. The intensity and concentration are high. In this particular competition I noticed that our tempos were way too fast, or at least faster than how we usually practiced. Yet, I was in awe of my fellow pipers who somehow managed to keep pace. I didn't hear many note mistakes, even from myself.

Standing in our circle, all of our eyes were on the pipe major's hands. This was to help with timing as well as notes. I wasn't even aware of the judges who were walking intimidatingly around the outside of the circle intently marking down comments on their clipboards. In fact, an earthquake could not have broken my concentration.

When we finished, the familiar sense of relief and pride enveloped me, and I wanted to rush to the pipe major and give him a huge hug. But decorum prevailed and we marched off—with a little extra sway to our kilts. Receiving second place failed to dampen our spirits, though we felt we had had a good chance at first. There was always "next year."

We did, indeed, return to Santa Rosa the next year for another try. We had struggled all summer with less than stellar results, though we knew we should have fared better than we'd had. There were perhaps 14 bands in our grade this particular year. We had drawn the straw to play last—usually not a good place to be. The judges are worn out, and the players have sunk into a malaise of a long afternoon. However, we were determined.

We marched up to the line and awaited the signal. The sound was good; we were off to a good start. As we played on, confidence increased. We were able to maintain good tempos, tuning and stage presence. We played well. As we marched off, one piper overheard a judge say, "And the last shall be first."

We realized we could have misheard and didn't want to hold out hope. But when the winners were announced, we had, indeed, reached the top of the ladder. Sweet success!

Inspired by the 1960s movie "Zulu," about an African tribe fighting the British in South Africa, Andrew had improvised a version of a Zulu chant for the band to yell during moments of victory. It was a gloriously "in your face" chant that we would yell whenever we got first place. To the uninitiated, Scottish bagpipe band members screaming a Zulu war chant at the top of their lungs might have seemed a bit strange. To our band, this was normal behavior. And, this particular night, there was a lot of beer flowing as well!

Descriptions of our experiences in Santa Rosa, California, would not be complete without mention of the port-o-potty caper. This incident from the 1990s may still be bantered about in bagpipe circles. At the end of one day's stressful competitions, all 40 or so bands marched onto the field for the final "Massed Bands" celebration.

> They vigorously pushed the port-o-potty from side to side as the hapless drummer was trapped inside.

Standing, usually in the hot sun, after a day of solo and band competitions sometimes was a real test of devotion for band members. While listening to all the announcements and introductions of people "who made this all possible," and other lengthy orations, the bands waited in anticipation of the announcements of the winners.

One of our members, during the interminable waiting, decided he could not wait any longer for one of nature's calls. The only option was a nearby port-o-potty off to the side but facing the large crowd in the stands. He jogged over as unobtrusively as possible. Two of our band members took one look at each other and, without saying a word, rushed over as he entered the small structure.

They then vigorously pushed the port-o-potty from side to side with the hapless drummer trapped inside. The crowd, who had been observing all of this in consternation, now roared its approval. The resident of the port-o-potty exited, obviously none too happy, as the two pranksters rushed back to their formation with the band. He had gained unwelcome notoriety forever.

ESTES PARK, COLORADO

The other big competition of the season took place in "Little Scotland"—Estes Park, Colorado, the gateway to Rocky Mountain National Park. These games are nationally recognized and are a complete games with a parade, Scottish athletics, dogs, vendors, general Scottish entertainment, dancing, and clan gatherings in addition to bagpipe competitions. Inspiring pipers to greater performances are 13-14,000-foot peaks in the distance already dotted with the first sprinkling of fall snow. Lending authenticity to a Scottish scene is the notorious Estes Park weather in September.

Colorado has beautiful fall weather—except for this particular weekend in Estes Park, year after year. Mother

Nature invariably decides to use this weekend as a warning that summer is over. Every year, the temperature can dependably drop to less than 50°F. and healthy wind gusts blow down from the mountains at unexpected times for unexpected durations. The gusts are frequently accompanied by spitting snow, rain or sleet. Sometimes there may be a combination of all three.

And in between squalls, just to keep the paying customers guessing, the intense sun may come out and warm things up nicely. I've seen morning blizzards turn into sunny 90° F. afternoons. As soon as the sweaters come off, another wind gust will whip up the kilts and convince the crowd they should spend some time at the Scotch-tasting tent.

A particularly impressive solo competition effort was observed one year at the Estes Park games. The weather was unsettled from the start. As an accomplished piper played a 15 minute piobaireachd, the classical music of the pipes, in front of an unflappable curmudgeon of a judge sitting under a small open tent to keep sun, rain or snow off (whichever applied at the moment), the tune was going well enough to attract attention. The few listeners nearby could feel a special performance in the offing.

As the tune unfolded and was molded, more and more of the surrounding crowd fell silent. I could feel the music flow through my body. After perhaps five minutes of the long "Lament for Donald of Laggan," and with the piper slowly and majestically walking back and forth in front of the judge, a sudden gust of wind tore into the games area.

The tent above the judge started to slowly flap in the growing breeze. In mere moments, the gust grew to a gale and intermittent rain turned to sleet. Papers flew, tables and chairs took to the air, and nearby people grabbed the judge's tent, which was ready to take flight. The piper was undeterred and played on, totally concentrated on the tune. He continued walking back and forth until he realized that the wind had become so strong that if he turned, the wind would blow his drones off his shoulders. I looked up to see that the piper's slow methodic pacing had stopped. The inspired piper was walking backward to a point just in front of the judge. The judge didn't move a muscle; the piper played on.

Spectators who rushed to hold the tent in place were struggling. Five bystanders were enlisted to keep the tent from blowing away and ruining a performance that still continued unflawed and uninterrupted.

The wind abated and the judge nodded acknowledgment when the tune finished. And was even heard to mutter, "Well done." The piper should have received first place just for the extra challenge.

Unfortunately, he had missed one note, and one note only, and, thus, came in second! I may be biased since the piper in question here was my husband, Andrew.

The band attended other Highland games in other parts of the country through the years: Salt Lake City, Atlanta, and Jackson (Wyoming) with varying results. By the year 2000, we were ready for the big time. Scotland or Bust!

24

BRINGING COALS TO NEWCASTLE

*At the climax of the music, a man dropped to his knees,
gathered his two young children in his arms and held
them tightly.*

One day, our band received a general notice, which had gone out to as many bagpipe bands around the world as possible, that a huge Millennium Parade for the year 2000 was being planned for Edinburgh, Scotland. The organizers' goal was to celebrate the millennium by attracting at least 10,000 pipers and drummers and putting on the biggest bagpipe parade in history. In addition, money would be raised for the Marie Curie Cancer Care.

Set for August 2000, the timing enabled bands to participate in several local Scottish competitions scheduled near that time. And one of our band members had indicated that American bands could arrange small shows in towns to entertain the locals. Talk about bringing coals to Newcastle! A bagpipe band in Scotland was certainly no big thing, but our ensuing interaction with the town elders and general residents in these towns would be a highlight of our visit. Andrew encouraged us to participate in a once-in-a-lifetime experience.

Masochistically, I took it upon myself to arrange the logistics for the entire trip. The group included fifty plus band members and their spouses, friends, children, and other band groupies traveling to Scotland. Of course, some wanted to leave Denver earlier or later than the group at large or wanted to join us on the way, or found some other way to put a fly in the ointment. By the time we left, I was lucky to have any hair left on my head.

We had contacted several Scottish municipalities to see if they had any interest in hosting an American bagpipe band. As if they hadn't heard bagpipes before? What were we thinking? Surprisingly, several responded quite positively. We sent a special offer to Dunblane, an attractive village north of Edinburgh, near Stirling Castle. We had a bittersweet connection to this town. Several years before, in 1996, Dunblane had been the site of an incomprehensible shooting of kindergartners by a madman. After killing sixteen innocent schoolchildren, one teacher, and wounding several others, the killer committed suicide.

By a quirk of fate, our band had a couple of dancers who had been students at Columbine High School in Littleton, Colorado, on that awful day when two students attacked the school and killed 12 students and one teacher in 1999, the year before we arrived in Scotland. One dancer was Andrew's daughter who, by a stroke of good fortune, had gone home for lunch that day, at the very time when the shootings started. Because Dunblane and our band shared tragedies that entwined us in a very special way, we offered to do a performance for them.

All the bands in the Denver area had been invited to play at the Columbine memorial service. A week after the shootings, we gathered in the large park designated for the memorial near the stage where the vice-president of the United States, Al Gore, and other dignitaries were to speak. As the thousands of mourners quietly and slowly made their way into the park, the noise level was eerily muffled.

At the appropriate time, we played "Amazing Grace," a common tune for such an occasion. That day it created more of an impact than usual. The shock of the shootings was still fresh, but the music brought some welcome release. It was an honor to be able to provide some solace for the people of Littleton who struggled to make sense of it all.

The city fathers of Dunblane accepted our proposal to visit. The town cleared the streets of cars and any traffic and made plans for us to march through the curvy, cobblestoned, narrow lanes. We were to finish the parade in front of Dunblane's impressive 13th century cathedral. As we formed a semi-circle in front of this towering edifice, the townspeople gathered to listen.

Robert Mathieson, of the Schotts and Dykehead Pipe Band, had written a beautiful tune in memory of those ill-fated children called the "Bells of Dunblane." Our band had included it for the memorial service for the Columbine students in Littleton, Colorado. We now shared it with the Dunblane populace.

As we were playing this moving tune, our large, burly drum major noticed a man in the crowd who, at the climax of the music, dropped to his knees, gathered his two young children in his arms and held them tightly. At that point, the tears freely flowed down our drum major's cheeks, and the pipers did all they could to hold themselves together. We had practiced the tune inside the cathedral before our walk commenced, which had more than humbled us. That practice had helped to settle us down and prepare us for the intense emotions felt during the day.

The townspeople then took us to the town hall where they had all sorts of tasty, handmade pastries and snacks for us. We chatted with these wonderfully hospitable people and shared our stories. We felt honored when they then guided us to the cemetery where a special memorial had been erected for the children. By then it was dusk, and we were played out, emotionally and physically. But never was there to be another day like that one.

We had begun the day by visiting Stirling Castle. Upon prior arrangement, we were to gather our band with our Highland dancers and march into the castle and play some musical sets on the castle grounds in front of whatever tourists happened to be in attendance.

Stirling Castle represents what castles should look like. Situated up on Castle Hill (an "intrusive crag," according to Wikipedia), towering above the surrounding area, steep cliffs on three sides, its stony towers and turrets date from the 15th and 16th

Stirling Castle provided a wonderful venue for my band.

centuries. A better setting for a bagpipe band would be difficult to find. We were received well by the audience and felt like we belonged there.

Highlighting our visit to Scotland was, of course, the Millennium Parade. Organizing 10,000 independent pipers and drummers into one large group was somebody's idea of pure masochism.

Divided into waves of 100 to 150, the pipe bands mixed and matched with other pipe bands from around the world. There may have been ten different bands in one wave.

Of course, the majority of bands came from Britain, but bands from Australia, Switzerland, France, and other countries one doesn't normally associate with bagpipes were in attendance as well. Bands gathered in side streets to form up and march down the Royal Mile from Edinburgh Castle to the Princes Street Gardens below. Some thoughtful organizer realized marching down and not up the rather steeply inclining cobblestoned street was a much better idea!

The extensive, lovely gardens, which looked up at the castle, set in a valley between the old and new towns, would then host a competition of bands desirous of

> The Millennium Parade had 10,000 independent pipers and drummers.

testing their mettle against bands in their same grade from around the world.

Wave after wave, the bands came, playing … who knows what? The bands had been mailed some common tunes to learn, though individual bands had their own settings to some of these tunes and

10,000 bagpipers and drummers filled the streets of Edinburgh
in the 2000 Millennium parade. (photo by Colin Dickson).

were hesitant to change just for the sake of unity in a
cacophonous conglomeration of bands.

The streets were lined with eager massive crowds who
could have cared less what the bands were playing or even
if they were in tune. The electricity in the air, the sound of
pipes and drums filling the city, the myriad colors of the
hundreds of different tartans overwhelmed the senses! My

stomach was churning with pride and tears flowed freely, realizing I was a part of something so moving.

The bands were allowed some lunchtime after the parade and before the competitions started. Our band gathered at a classic pub and rubbed elbows with members of other bands from everywhere.

After some bangers and mash, saving the beer for after the competition, our band retired to the massive gardens, searching for our grade's competition area. This would be our first competition in the mother country. "Intimidation" doesn't even begin to describe our jittery approach. There may have been 20 bands in our grade. And these were from countries that were far more versed in the vagaries of bagpipe competition than we would ever be.

We found our spot, checked into the games with the judge, and proceeded to tune up. On the outside, we appeared calm and professional; inside, we were a mass of jelly. Finally, it was time for us to form up in our columns to march into our circle to be judged by real Scottish judges leering over their clipboards

... indeed, Prince Charles was in front of the audience listening to our tunes!

eager to write their cryptic comments, good and bad. Tension was high.

It was at that moment that Andrew, our pipe major, turned to the band and said, "You all don't mind if Prince Charles just walked onto the field, do you?" We all nervously laughed thinking Andrew was just making a joke trying to get us to relax.

The command was given. We struck up our pipes

Prince Charles in background enjoyed our band's first ever Scottish competition.

and marched into our competition circle. I happened to look beyond Andrew about ten yards and was astonished to see that, indeed, Prince Charles was in front of the audience listening to our tunes! Andrew had not been kidding; he had been alerting us to a real situation. I quickly refocused on our pipe major's fingers on his chanter, figuring I really didn't need anything else to distract me. We completed our tunes and marched off, feeling we had played well.

While we were congratulating ourselves, the prince walked over to interact with the colonials. He was quite approachable and amiable. We all chatted up a bit. I was in the background a ways, holding in my hand my shoes, which had been killing me. For some reason, Prince Charles chose that time to reach out and shake my hand in a congenial, friendly manner. Caught by surprise, I realized that I hadn't the foggiest idea of how to address a prince, particularly with shoes in my hand.

I'm usually not at a loss for words, but the best I could do was some unintelligible stuttering. Mercifully, he turned away without comment. I don't think I really had anything specifically to say to him anyway. "How's Camilla?" probably wouldn't have hit the right note. Still, I should have come up with an appropriate remark. Now I'm thinking I'd better brush up on how to address a prince, but chances are I've blown my one and only opportunity.

We were scheduled to compete in the actual World Championships in Glasgow a week or so later. Though we were only a grade IV band, we would have the chance to hear the big boys in grades I and II. After playing our best and realizing we weren't really in the running, we ambled over to the area of the higher-level competitions.

Most of the crowd elbowed their way close to the front of the circle to get a good vantage point. Band after band marched into the circle and, to our ears, played flawlessly. I once asked a judge who was a friend how on earth he managed to rank Grade I bands. He said he just prayed for a mistake.

The day was special but couldn't live up to the Millennium March, the Stirling Castle or Dunblane experiences. The day lost more of its luster when we stood in formation for more than an hour in a growing Scottish drizzle listening to announcements and finally the awards.

Our band would compete in a couple of other games, acquitting ourselves well enough for an American band. Since that time, bands from the United States have become more recognized and accepted and have actually earned some good prizes. But, in 2000, we were introducing Colorado to the home country.

We also had arranged for a show in Oban, a lovely small town on the Firth of Lorn on the west coast of Scotland. As our bus entered the sleepy tourist town, the town officials eagerly met us, happy we had been able to make our appointed date.

Because Oban is known as the "seafood capital of Scotland," the dockside is an important gathering place in town. Ferries leave there for the famous Isle of Skye, and tourist shops fill the streets. This is where we were to entertain passers-by. Our dancers were always able to draw a crowd, and, again, the crowd was appreciative.

The town elders then showed us what Scottish hospitality really meant. We were taken to a restaurant overlooking the bay and all 50 of us were fed a scrumptious lunch! Presenting us with Oban neckties commemorating the town as well as a special plaque dedicated to our visit, the town officials could not have been more congenial, gracious and generous.

Our show went over so well that they requested that we repeat it in the afternoon. We were only too happy to oblige and gathered two hours later at the same dockside. Without the distractions of competition, we thoroughly enjoyed being able to bring pleasure to those listening.

A postscript to the day came a month later. Andrew, as pipe major, received a letter from an unknown source. It came from a tourist who had been in Oban that day, enjoying McCaig's Tower, a monument reminiscent of the

Roman Coliseum, though on a considerably smaller scale. Located high above town, this area provides spectacular views of the town and bay.

It apparently also provides a great place to hear a bagpipe band on the dock! The author of the letter described hearing the distant bagpipes from this vantage point and being incredibly moved to have such an added attraction to his visit. He had somehow tracked down not only the name of our band but our address as well.

He had enjoyed the pipes so much that he had taken the time to ensure that we knew we had created some real joy for him. Andrew replied how much his letter meant to us, and we realized that, beyond all things, bringing such pleasure to others was our highest purpose. As Andrew stated at one point, "Here lies our chief virtue: we have the power and the gift to bring happiness—even if it's only for a short time—into the lives of others."

Several years before the big band trip to the mother country, Andrew and I had ventured across the sea to Ireland and Scotland, countries of our heritages. We had brought one set of bagpipes knowing we would only play to ourselves when the mood arose.

We chose special places appropriate enough: in Ireland, we found castle ruins and the Cliffs of Moher, which stand 700 feet above the surf, running about five miles long, perhaps the closest geologic formation from Europe to the U.S. Windswept and barren, there is not a more inspiring spot to play to the gods. Okay, so there are a lot of inspiring places to play bagpipes. We would stop at various picturesque spots, break out the pipes, and enjoy communing with the deities.

Andrew, however, was looking for new horizons. Many instruments have passed through his hands through the years; he is an excellent pianist and plays the autoharp with bluegrass bands. He also enjoys karaoke singing. Somewhere along the way he learned to play the spoons. We were in Nova Scotia and landed at "The Red Barn" to hear a world-class spoon player who offered Andrew a set of spoons and a short lesson when Andrew cornered him at the intermission.

We also have garnered about five or six didgeridoos along the way. He especially enjoyed playing these for my 7th grade geography students when we studied Australia. Both of us have recently become enamored with the Swiss alphorn and are learning how to play.

Never understanding quite how his brain works, I marveled at his insistence that we stop at a hardware store during our travels in Ireland. He returned to the car shortly with a five-foot piece of PVC pipe and some beeswax and paint. Shaking my head, I could only surmise one thing: he planned to turn this into a didgeridoo. In fact, PVC pipe does a credible job of imitating a real didgeridoo made from a eucalyptus tree. But now that he had it, I had no idea exactly how he planned to use it.

That night in the motel he added a mouthpiece to the PVC/didgeridoo. Shortly thereafter, we stopped at an old ruined fort practically buried out of sight into earthen works. We toured the perimeter, not really knowing what we were looking at. Upon our return to the car, we passed a field with cows quietly munching. Andrew was always fond of telling a story about some Scottish Angus cows he drove by many years before in California. His passenger, an elderly aunt, remarked on the cows and insisted Andrew prove his claim that Angus cows displayed a special reaction to bagpipes.

Backed into a corner, Andrew stopped the car and took out his pipes. He claims to this day, with his aunt's confirmation, that upon the first note, the cows jerked their heads up from grazing and ran directly to him. They formed a semi-circle around him and stared, with rapt attention clearly written on their faces. When he finished his last note, they wandered off and returned to their grazing.

Now, in Ireland, he would conduct a similar test with Irish cows and the didgeridoo. He slipped the didgeridoo over the wooden fence and bleeped out the one note didges play. Sure enough, the cows lifted their heads and walked purposefully toward the sound. Again, the cows formed a semi-circle as they seemed enraptured with the sound. One particularly assertive cow walked right up to the didgeridoo and actually stuck her tongue up the pipe! Clearly, she was enjoying the music in a very special way. Who knows what was on her mind!

We slipped over to Scotland and particularly sought out the standing stones that abound in Scotland. We made sure we played at Boreraigh, the birthplace of the premier Scottish piping school on the Isle of Skye. It was founded by the famous MacCrimmons, the hereditary pipers for the MacLeods of Dunvegan. We also played among the Callanish Stones, standing stones arranged in a circle, reminiscent of Stonehenge, which were a focus in the Bronze Age on the Isle of Lewis in the Outer Hebrides.

Timing was everything. We learned that tourists clear out from most popular tourist areas by early evening. We timed our visits to coincide with their exodus so that we could enjoy these places in peace and quiet. This was also true in the famous Glencoe area on the mainland. Perhaps the most famous glen in Scotland, this unique spot is filled with ghosts and eeriness as well as beauty. This was the site of the infamous Glencoe Massacre committed by the Campbells on the MacDonalds in the late 1600s.

Though details have been conveniently clouded over the years, the general story is that the MacDonalds, in true traditional Scottish hospitality, gave refuge to the Campbells, in spite of much enmity between the two clans. The rules of Scottish hospitality at that time dictated that if you gave refuge to someone, then that person would enjoy complete safety in your home, even if he were your mortal enemy. In the wee hours of the morning, the Campbells rose up and slew 38 of the MacDonalds.

The persisting tension has had a difficult time dying. In fact, we saw a truck with the name "Campbell's Moving and Storage" broken down on the high end of the road. The Campbells are not well thought of even to this day, and we suspect the truck might still be there.

As we drove through the popular tourist attraction, we saw cars, buses, and camera-laden sightseers all over the road photographing anything that moved or didn't. The atmosphere was a little Coney Island-ish. We stopped but not for long. We couldn't get in the mood and continued on to the next town. We checked into a small inn with the notice on the front desk, "Campbells unwelcome."

After dinner and a pint, we returned to the middle of the glen and pulled off in a lovely spot without a person in sight. The reds, mauves, burnt browns, and faded yellows covering the heathered landscape rose in slowly sweeping barren hills. Paranormal shadows and a cool breeze invited us to walk away from the road. The sun was slowly setting adding a hazy, diffuse light. We walked without talking, enveloping ourselves into the glen.

It was Andrew's turn to take out the pipes and play a special piobaireachd called "The Massacre of Glencoe." The slow, roughly ten minute piece accurately reflects the ignominious actions of that terrible massacre. I'm sure that classical piece has been played there many times, but this particular evening was ours. Such moments as these are the highlights of a piper's life.

Moving on up the coast, we stopped at a bed & breakfast inn near the water. The rocky beach called to me, but as I stepped over a rickety fence designed to keep people from doing just what I was doing, I tripped and somersaulted down a rock pile, somehow avoiding a broken head. Unfortunately I did severely sprain my knee. As I gimped along the street in the nearby town the next day, I spied a cane I could use to help me continue our wanderings. Hobbling down the street, I passed a familiar face!

Andrew played "Battle of Glencoe" in the Glencoe Valley of Scotland.

The previous year a few bagpipers were invited to play at the Telluride Bluegrass Music Festival in Colorado as part of an encore by the Wolfstone Band. I had never heard of this band, but when they took the stage at 11:00 p.m. after a very lengthy Bela Fleck bluegrass concert, people began filtering out of the amphitheater. However, upon hearing the first notes, the crowd, practically as a whole, returned to the stage area to hear this Scottish band that played a folk/rock mix.

Complete with a bagpiper, the band was upbeat and had grabbed the audience by the second bar. As I listened, I was humbled to think we would actually be playing with them. We were to join them on just one encore tune, which we'd received previously. We practiced that afternoon with their bagpiper.

The old butterflies were felt as we gathered backstage for a last cursory tuning. The band began their encore with a slow mournful fiddle; the keyboard and guitars joined slowly one by one. Then the key changed and the pipers walked onstage. Even before we joined in, the crowd went wild. The result was nothing short of pandemonium.

As we finished the tune with the pipes dominating, the affect of the music on the crowd was overwhelming; it showed me why musicians become addicted to performing. The incessant screaming, clapping and whistling indicated they were ready to tear their clothes off. We took our bows with the band and were amazed at such a reception after playing only one tune.

So, now here I was in Fort William, Scotland, gamely trying to use my cane to walk down the street. As I crept along, I recognized one of the band members from Wolfstone! I gasped some sort of greeting and reminded him of our meeting in Telluride. Here was one of those chance encounters that give rise to the "small world" label. We chatted a bit and we realized I would be playing with their band again in a month at the bluegrass festival in Lyons, Colorado.

As if that wasn't enough of a coincidence, I continued down the street, following the strains of the familiar sound of a bagpipe. As I caught up to the fellow who was busking, trying to earn a bit of extra cash on the street, I realized his face was familiar, too. Not more than three months earlier, I had been walking down the Pearl Street Mall in Boulder and heard the bagpipe sound.

Here on the streets of Fort William I ran into this same bagpiper! Fellow pipers had found one another again—not hard if one of you is actually playing. So, here in Fort William, we recounted our meeting in Boulder, said something about that small world thing, and went on our ways.

Andrew and I headed to Glasgow to spend more than two hours in a special bagpipe shop where he must have blown every chanter in the place. Finally satisfied with one that met his incredibly high standards, we reached the National Piping Center and its museum only to find the doors closed! Like I said, timing is everything. As we flew home, we had no idea we would be returning several years later with our entire band.

EPILOGUE

My involvement with bagpipes was "a good ride," as they say, and I wouldn't have missed it for the world. I still get goose bumps when I hear the strains of bagpipes.

After our heady experience in Scotland with our band and one more rousing weekend in Sidney, Nebraska, Andrew and I made a bittersweet decision and retired from piping. We rode off into the sunset to enjoy more of life than just bagpipes. Being a member of the band, and, in Andrew's case, being the pipe major, was all consuming. Not only were we dealing with an impossible instrument, but also unique people with a wide variety of personalities, both endearing and frustrating. After 15 years for me and 30 plus years for Andrew, we were ready to move on. Bagpiping and our bagpipe band would always be in our hearts.

I continued to travel and considered sharing my pipes with other interesting cultures. I regret not taking them to Nepal and Thailand, but I was not sure that the locals would have fond memories of British imperialism and decided against it. Nor did I want to encumber our porters in Nepal with any more than they already were carrying for us.

My small group of five fellow teachers trekked up through the Annapurna Sanctuary to the base of the Annapurnas. Starting out from Pokara at less than 3,000 feet and spending five or more days to reach 13,000+ feet did not seem daunting at all, especially to someone who lived in Colorado and had climbed many of the 14,000 foot peaks. When I reached our goal, I would be gazing up at several peaks in the Annapurna Range of more than 22,000 feet.

What had not been clear was that this was no gradual ascent. The "trail" was a lot of steep uphill only to be followed by a lot of steep downhill. The amount of elevation gained and lost was considerable. So we logged in far more than 12,000 feet of total gain. Most of it was in barely tolerable heat and humidity; it was just at the beginning of the monsoon season.

I carried only water and a rain jacket in my daypack. But any pride had been totally dissipated on day five when one of the porters offered to take even that, and, with ill concealed enthusiasm, I said, "Yes!" Oh, the ignominy! I couldn't imagine what I would have done with bagpipes. And, of course, the location most calling for pipes was at the base of the Annapurnas at almost 14,000 feet. If I had had trouble playing on Mt. Fuji at 12,388 feet, Annapurna would have been an impossible challenge.

Our group flew on to Khandbari, the hometown of our trip sponsor, who now lived in Boulder. We were to visit the Surya School he had built and interact with fellow teachers. After briefly settling into his family's house on the main street, we proceeded to the school.

As we carefully descended the steps from town to the school, hundreds of students were out to greet us with clapping and heaps of flowers thrust into our hands. After some introductions, our trip leader formally presented the considerable amount of educational supplies we had brought, including an impressive speaker system and special books for the English-speaking students. Their gratitude was shown in a talent show they gave us a few days later, which lasted more than three hours in the hot sun. We appreciated the efforts, nonetheless.

We then spread out to classrooms of our various grade levels to what we thought would be an observation. As I walked into the 7th grade room with 20 or so students, I realized there was no teacher in sight. The eager students were quietly sitting waiting for the return of their teacher who was taking a break in the faculty room.

As I walked in and introduced myself, they insisted that I teach. "Teach us! Teach us!" they clamored. How can a teacher resist? I had absolutely no supplies or lesson plans with me, and the classroom had only one sad looking blackboard up front. Winging it, I drew an outline of the world on the board, and we reviewed what they knew about continents and countries.

Coming to the close of that activity, it became apparent I was still to be on stage. I always believed in activity in the classroom, so I pounced on the idea of teaching these bright-eyed, grateful students a Scottish Highland dance. With no bagpipes or electricity for a tape player for music, I was reduced to singing a dance tune as we hopped around and giggled. I would find myself in other classrooms doing the same thing. In one classroom, the students spontaneously all joined in singing the tune as they danced! Yes, I would have liked to have had my bagpipes then.

A few years later, I was able to obtain a partial scholarship to visit southern Africa with a group sponsored by the Denver Zoo. It seemed obvious to me that a safari was not the place for bagpipes. I'm pretty sure the pipes not only would not have attracted any animals, they would have cleared the region of any animals we hoped to see. Or, thinking about the alternative, I could have been voraciously attacked after the first notes! I could only imagine what the claws of lions would do to a bagpipe bag!

Hiking trips to Europe, Alaska and Canada were logistically complicated enough without the extra baggage of bagpipes. Further, Europeans and North Americans were more than familiar with bagpipes; the opportunity to introduce bagpipes to different cultures was missing. I did travel to Peru later and the idea of playing them at Machu Picchu was appealing, but I wanted to respect the Incan traditions in such an incomparably spiritual place. Bagpipes there would have seemed an intrusion, so I left them at home.

My involvement with bagpipes was "a good ride," as they say, and I wouldn't have missed it for the world. My life is so much richer for having been a bagpiper. Sadly, my bagpipes languish in a bagpipe bag in a corner of the guest bedroom now. I pull them out only on rare occasions when friends ask for a special playing. But, like so many things, "If you don't use it, you lose it." For all the struggle and frustration I experienced to learn how to play the pipes, I could never have foreseen the day when they would gather dust.

However, Andrew and I have moved on to learning the alphorn, the 12-foot long horn, particular to Switzerland, Germany, and Austria, best recognized from the old Ricola TV ads. Another great challenge is ahead of us. And, to our relief, there are no marching alphorn bands!

Will I take my alphorn to different countries and introduce the sound to other cultures? Even though the large horns can separate into three parts, the package is still quite bulky. While the idea is appealing, the practicality is not there. I don't believe I could ever replicate the experiences I've had with my bagpipes.

Our newest musical challenge is the Swiss alphorn.

Will I ever pick up the pipes again and rejoin a band?
I'm old enough to know not to say, "Never." I still get goose
bumps when I hear the strains of bagpipes. Fond memories
of all the experiences and encounters I had playing the
pipes well up. And the pipes still stir my soul. Who knows?

Andrew and Susan spent many happy years in the
City of Denver Pipe Band.

ACKNOWLEDGMENTS

This book would not have come to fruition without the moral and physical assistance of my husband, Andrew. As the pipe-major of our bagpipe band and my mentor, he helped instill a love of the incomparable, challenging music of the bagpipes. He was also an invaluable bagpipe teacher. His more than many suggestions on my written form of the book made it a reality.

Members of my City of Denver Pipe Band, (too many to name) saw me through many personal as well as band troubles and struggles. Without their support, I would have lost my confidence early on learning how to play the bagpipes. My first bagpipe teacher, Mark Ryan, saw desire in me and started me on my journey. Many instructors at the bagpipe school in Coeur d'Alene (Andrew Wright, Evan McCrea, Alan Walters, and Albert Duncan) also encouraged my further endeavors with the pipes. All the bagpipers who have shared their music with budding pipers such as myself provided incomparable inspiration.

Judith Briles, The Book Shepherd, guided me by the hand to understand the world of writing and publishing books. The ultimate guru in her field, Judith's patient explanations, many workshops, monthly meetings, innumerable books and personal support were essential in making it all work.

Sallie Greenwood, John Maling, Judith Briles and Peggie Ireland were invaluable and able to decipher my intentions and turn them into a readable form. Nick Taylor and Nick Zelinger made the book into a real creation, pleasing to read and enjoy. And Kelly Johnson of Cornerstone Virtual Assistance offered incomparable help and moral support to my technological struggles. Nick Zelinger helped to create a pleasing back of the book.

My fellow travelers, the good, the bad, the ugly—and the beautiful—all contributed in making my traveling more interesting and memorable, if not frustrating at times. The guides, Smoke Blanchard and Dewey Webster, managed and herded my groups in a safe and competent manner under conditions that would try most mortal men.

Dewey also contributed some wonderful photographs.

Many friends supported me throughout the process, mentally and logistically: Sallie Greenwood, John Auld, and Barbara McKee. They helped more than they know.

Writing a book is an emotional endeavor, which can move your soul. I appreciated all the help that made it happen.

ABOUT THE AUTHOR

Susan Planck is as unique as the bagpipe. With her background as an elementary, middle, and high school teacher for 30 years, with more than 30 different subjects under her command, she also captivated children and adults as a bagpipe teacher and climbing school instructor for 15 years.

Attaining a lifelong dream of learning how to play the bagpipes shortly before she turned 40, Susan enjoyed sharing the incredible, strange sounds of the bagpipes during her many travels to foreign countries. She found nirvana combining her two loves, traveling and bagpiping.

Moving to Colorado, she joined the City of Denver Bagpipe Band, an award-winning band that competed throughout the United States and Scotland. She quickly learned that bagpiping would change her life in ways never anticipated, including meeting her husband who was the pipe-major of the band.

Susan resides in Boulder with her husband, Andrew. They now spend their time mastering the Swiss alphorn.

I enjoyed taking you on my travels into the world of bagpiping and abroad to interesting locations around the world. If you have enjoyed this book, in any way, please be so kind as to write a review by clicking on *Piping Hot!* on Amazon.com.

To learn more about Susan please visit:

plancksusan@gmail.com

SusanPlanck.com

facebook.com/susan.planck